The Gifted Kids Survival Guide

The Gifted Kids Survival Guide

Judy Galbraith

Free Spirit™
PUBLISHING

ISBN: 0-915793-01-6

Free Spirit Publishing Company
123 North Third Street
Suite 716
Minneapolis, MN 55401
(612) 338-2068

Library of Congress Catalog Card Number: 84-80997

Galbraith, Judy, 1954-
    The gifted kids survival guide
    1. Gifted children. 2. Education. 3. Title

Printed in the United States of America

15   14   13   12   11   10

Also by Judy Galbraith: THE GIFTED KIDS SURVIVAL GUIDE
                        (For Ages 10 & Under)
                        Free Spirit Publishing Company
                        ISBN: 0-915793-00-8

To the gifted kids I've worked with (you know who you are) who made teaching magically memorable. And to those GTs I haven't met, I hope this book, in some small way, helps you to be all you can be.

Table of Contents

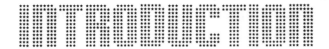

INTRODUCTION

This is a very unusual book.

Instead of being a book *about* gifted kids, it's a book *for* gifted kids.

Not only is it a book *for* gifted kids, instead of about them, it also takes sides — yours.

But rather than waste a lot of time with a book that may or may not be meant for you, we'll tell you straight off what it's about *and* what it isn't about.

First, a few notes about what this book *is* for:

The Gifted Kids Survival Guide was written with the help of over 300 GT* teenagers. Together we'll help you do a number of important things:

---

*Many gifted kids told us they don't like the label "gifted." Some felt more comfortable with talented. So we've shortened gifted/talented to GT and will use that abbreviation throughout the book.

- **Solve** the Eight Great Gripes of gifted kids
- **Get a better deal** in school — make it more fun, challenging
- **Learn why** you need more freedom, more responsibility
- **Reduce stress** related to being GT
- **Improve relations** with your parent(s)
- **Quit trying to be perfect** and start enjoying your giftedness
- **Make friends** with kids (and adults) who really understand you
- **Set realistic goals** that both you and your parents can live with
- **Charge up your motivation** to get things done.
- **Stick up** for your rights

You'll learn from the successful experiences of hundreds of GT teenagers interviewed for this book, from forward-thinking teachers, from parents who know and *understand* what it's like to parent gifted kids.

For starters, you're going to learn about who's gifted and why: how they got that way, and who said so. You'll be able to see in what ways *you* are gifted.

If you want school to be more meaningful, more challenging, we'll show you how to take the system by the horns and make changes in *your* favor.

Gifted kids tell us that problems with school are their #1 concern. It's no wonder either. Most school courses are designed for average learners — whoever they are. (More on that later.) We'll show you what can and is being done to challenge bright students like yourself. We'll show you how to gain greater control over your education through proper planning and action. And you'll learn straight from GTs themselves as they share their school stories.

If you want teachers to have realistic expectations of you, this book will give you the ammunition you'll need to get the message across: that it's great to be smart — BUT YOU'RE NOT PERFECT! You have a right to bomb out just like everyone else. You have a right *not* to "live up to your potential" all the time if you don't want to.

You'll learn all about friends — GT teenagers' second most important concern. We'll show you how to make them, how to keep them, and how to be accepted without compromising mind, body or health. We'll also explain why others react to GTs the way they do. And we'll offer suggestions about how to tackle the single, most distressing problem between GTs and their peers: the truckloads of teasing you get about being good at what you do.

We'll chronicle the trials and tribulations of being part of a family and offer solid advice on how to handle the high expectations parents often have of their gifted children. We'll also explain what it's like to be the *parent* of a GT. In seeing things from their point of view, you'll be in a better position to negotiate positive changes in your relationship with them.

You've heard about stress in adult life? We'll talk about stress and GTs. Being exceptionally bright or talented can bring greater degrees of stress: with your teachers, friends, and family. And we'll show you what it is, and how to reduce it.

Finally, we'll give you the tools you'll need to gain control and get what you want out of life. The students that were most successful in making changes in school, home or with friends were assertive and had terrific goal-setting and problem-solving skills.

You can have those abilities too! Without them, you'll wind up hoping and *waiting* for a change which may never occur. We'll show you how to set goals and follow through with them. This section also will provide you with easy steps for assertiveness and problem solving in *any* area of your life.

In the Appendix, you'll find a list of resources to contact if you want more information about giftedness. We've also compiled a list of books and magazines of interest to many GTs.

APPENDIX

Mind Expanding Magazines

•

Recommended Reading

•

GT Organizations

•

Credits

**So much for what this book is.
Now, for what it isn't.**

First, it doesn't offer any easy solutions. In order to make the changes you feel are important, you may be asked to make waves, confront and question authority, reexamine your motives, your thinking and to otherwise rock the boat.

It doesn't promise to make you well, or solve all your problems. And that's because the choice is up to you. But believe us when we say, if you *want* to know more about giftedness, feel better about yourself, solve problems and create new opportunities, we'll show you how to do it.

It isn't preachy. It doesn't moralize. There are no shoulds, gottas, ought to's (well, maybe a few). If you want to try some of our suggestions, that's great! We hope we can help. But if you don't, that's O.K. too.

Sometimes, a few things we say will appear self-evident to you, even boringly apparent. But before you put down the suggestion - *try it*. No matter how plain or ordinary it might seem.

This is not the last word on the subject either. We're smart enough (and so are you) to know that if you don't find what you're looking for in this book, you'll keep on looking until you find it.

It's been said, and I agree, that life is a journey. I hope that, with the help of this book, your journey will be more than an exercise in survival. I hope your journey will be challenging, happy and fulfilling.

Peace,
Judy Galbraith

We are an intelligent species and the use of our intelligence quite properly gives us pleasure. In this respect the brain is like a muscle. When it is in use, we feel very good. Understanding is joyous.

— **Carl Sagan**

BEING TEEN

It is certainly no news to you that being a teenager can be a terribly frustrating experience. Sometimes it must seem that life is nothing but one problem after another — a steady stream of hassles too overwhelming to solve; too important to share with just anybody. And why bother? They probably wouldn't understand anyway.

Just look at this list, for example. Do any of these look familiar?

1. School is a drag.
2. My parents don't understand me; they're always on my case.
3. I don't understand my parents. I don't know what they want.
4. I wish I were more popular.
5. I'm not pretty (tall, short, thin...) enough.
6. I shouldn't smoke (or drink, or have sex or stay out late, or...)
7. I can't do what I want.
8. I don't know what I want to be when I grow up.
9. I think I might have VD.
10. Sometimes, I don't think anybody loves me.
11. My teachers are boring.
12. I never have any money.
13. My car is a piece of junk.
14. I don't like my clothes
15. _____
16. _____
17. _____

*Life is just one damned
thing after another.*

— Frank Ward O'Malley

And the list can go on and on. Sometimes you may get so fed up that you'll want to hang up the whole thing and drop out.

Actually, almost all kids have most of these problems, to one degree or another. They all worry about school, and drugs, their sexuality, and parents, and cars and other stuff.

But gifted kids have even more worries.

And that's what this book is about: the concerns shared by GT kids. They're made all the more important by the fact that unless they're dealt with, the problems can interfere with your giftedness, perhaps even permanently damage it.

And what are these problems?

The Eight Great
Gripes
of Gifted Kids

1. The stuff we do in school is too easy and it's boring.
2. Parents, (teachers, friends) expect us to be perfect, to "do our best" *all* the time.
3. Friends who really understand us are few and far between.
4. Lots of our coursework is irrelevant.
5. Peers often tease us about being smart.
6. We feel overwhelmed by the number of things we can do in life.
7. We feel too different, alienated.
8. We worry a lot about world problems and feel helpless to do anything about them.

You can probably add a few of your own:

1. _____
2. _____
3. _____
4. _____
5. _____

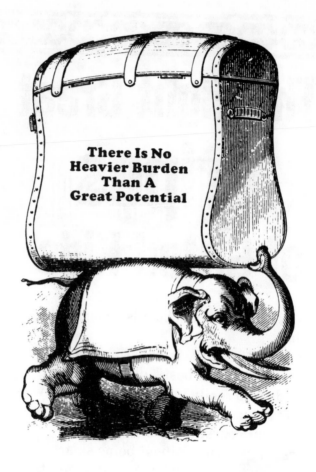

There Is No
Heavier Burden
Than A
Great Potential

These are the major problems that gifted teenagers tell us they face today—all issues that are the result of their exceptional abilities.

Isn't it a drag? Here you are with this outstanding potential which ironically can bring more hassles than happiness, more stress and anxiety than joy and refreshment.

Undoubtedly, some of these problems don't bug you now, but they may in the future. For example, you may find school challenging and your teachers terrific this year. But sometime in the future, you may find yourself in the opposite position.

For right now, though, I am sure you're experiencing enough of these gripes to make you feel this book was written just for you and you're right — it was.

RUGT?

The splendid achievements of the intellect,
like the soul, are everlasting.
— Sallust 86-34 B.C.

One of the most important questions you've probably asked yourself about being gifted is "what difference does it make anyway?"

I mean, just because you're intellectually brighter or can master computers or paint or dance or play an instrument exceptionally well, what difference does it make? Is that going to make you happier or richer or more successful or what?

In order to answer that question, you've first got to be able to answer the question what gifted is and is not. Then you can worry about whether it's good to be GT.

Myths about the gifted and talented

There are many misconceptions about what it means to be GT. We're sure you're familiar with some of them — you may even be able to add a few to our list:

Myth #1   Gifted kids have it made and will succeed in life *no matter what.*

Isn't it preposterous to think that just because someone is GT, life is going to be handed to them on a silver platter? Let's get serious! Everybody needs help and encouragement to make the most of themselves.

Myth #2   Gifted kids like school, *always* get good grades and greet each new school day with enthusiasm.

Most schools aren't set up for GTs. Schools are geared for average learners. Yet you're expected to stay there and cope. Several studies show that as many as 20 percent of our high school dropout population is gifted! What a waste.

Myth #3   Gifted students only come from white, middle to upper class families.

It might be easy to conclude that GTs come only from white, middle-class homes because the system often excludes people from minority cultures or those who have handicaps. In reality, GTs come from all ethnic and socio-economic backgrounds. They're also found among the handicapped and learning disabled.

Myth #4   Gifted kids are good at *everything.*

There may be a few people who appear to fit this description but only those related to Superman are good at everything.

Myth #5   Teachers can identify GTs and like to work with them.

Some can and some can't. Some do and some don't. There are a number of teachers who feel uncomfortable with GTs and get defensive because they may not know as much as the students do. Certain teachers equate giftedness with a student who is conforming, polite and gets good grades. These qualities are not synonymous with being GT.

Myth #6   If GTs are grouped together, they'll become snobs or elitist.

GTs don't *automatically* become snobs any more than other kids become snobs when they're grouped together. Some do — some don't. GTs who don't, recognize that being GT doesn't mean they're better than others, any more than being a member of a GT *group* promotes you to an elitist rank.

Myth #7   All gifted kids have trouble adjusting to school and friends.

Simply not true. While many GTs experience difficulties and face problems such as those presented in this book, there are others who are happy, and know how to get what they want from life.

Holly, 15, is a good example of a GT who is perceptive, self-assured and has good problem solving skills. She had this to say:

> "Some people think that all gifted kids are far-out basket cases. That all we do is read books and study. I was like that for awhile.
>
> "But I think a lot of us are pretty normal. We get good grades and are involved in extracurricular activities.
>
> "When I was in 7th and 8th grade, all I did was study. I got tired of my image. All people knew about me was that I got all A's and read a lot of books. I decided that I was the only one who could change things so I tried out for a school play and got a part. I realized that I could get up on a stage and perform. I got involved in choir. Now my grades aren't straight A's but I'm learning more things that are fun and will be helpful later in life."
>
> — Holly, 15

21

def′ə nish′ən

Has anyone ever told you what being gifted and talented means? Probably not. Or if they have it's likely the description was vague or confusing. That's because nobody can agree on a definition.

There are government definitions, school and teacher definitions, administrative definitions, researchers' and authors' definitions and dictionary definitions. And they're all different.

Let me show you what I mean.

Webster's Dictionary says: gift - ed (-id) adj. 1. having a natural ability or aptitude; 2. notably superior in intelligence.

gifted *adj* **1 :** endowed by nature or training with a gift: as **a :** having a special talent or other desirable quality ⟨~ with ... spontaneous ease and charm —Dorothy Sayers⟩ ⟨~ in making coffee or chicken salad —Agnes S. Turnbull⟩ ⟨so much in love with the word and so little ~ for the deed —Lewis Galantiere⟩ ⟨a ~ linguist⟩ **b :** having superior intellectual capacity usu. with an intelligence quotient in the genius class ⟨a ~ child⟩ **2 :** reflecting or revealing a special gift or talent **:** OUTSTANDING, NOTABLE ⟨had a ~ voice —Jean Stafford⟩ ⟨two novels ... were recognized as remarkably ~ —Time⟩ — **gift·ed·ly** *adv* — **gift·ed·ness** *n* -ES

Like all dictionary definitions, this one is predictably loose and leaves a great deal of the definition to your imagination. We all have natural abilities, for example. Does that mean we are all gifted? *How much more* intellectually superior than whom must you be to be considered gifted? I don't know. Do you?

WHAT THE FEDS SAY

As you might expect, the federal government has its definition, in order to set guidelines for identifying and educating GTs. In typical government gobbledygook it says:

> "gifted and talented children" means children and, whenever applicable, youth, who are identified at the preschool, elementary, or secondary level as possessing demonstrated or potential abilities that give evidence of high performance capability in areas such as intellectual, creative, specific academic, or leadership ability, or in the performing and visual arts, and who by reason thereof require services or activities not ordinarily provided by the school."

Whew! Now if you really want to know what all that means, here's a translation:

GT Ability	**Translation**
Intellectual ability	= the all-around smart person, somebody who's very good at most everything they apply themselves to.
Specific academic aptitude	= Someone who does exceptionally well in one or more particular subjects like math, science or history, etc.
Creative	= This person is known for thinking up unique solutions to problems, someone who does things in unconventional ways. (If you were stranded on a desert island, this is the kind of person you'd want to have along.)
Leadership	= Someone who's good at getting other people to do things. They like to organize and plan activities.
Visual and performing arts	= dancers who make it look easy, musicians who make it sound easy, artists of all varieties that have exceptional talent.

And here's still another definition — this one using that old bugaboo, IQ:

> Superior general intellectual potential and ability (approx. 120+ IQ). High functional ability to achieve in various academic areas commensurate with such intellectual ability; a high order talent in such areas as art, music, mechanical ability, foreign languages, science, math, drama, social leadership and creative writing; and a creative ability to develop a novel event in the environment.

Sounds pretty good, doesn't it? But this and all definitions have problems. They're either too restrictive or too general. And in human terms, somebody either gets included when maybe they shouldn't be — or worse yet, they get left out.

So much for what the "experts" think about what giftedness means. Here's how GT kids describe gifted and talented:

I think gifted is a good thing to be

Having a knack for subjects.

Giftedness is standing out because you're smarter.

Liking things that are different

Gifted is being smarter than most kids

Things come naturally when you're gifte

People have varying consciousness levels rather than varying intelligence levels

Somebody who excels in school on tests and things like that.

When you're gifted does that mean you're s'posed to get A's?

Gifted means creative, talented, interested in the happenings of the world.

Gifted could mean a lot of things; comprehending above your grade level, doing better than average, advanced.

I'm not sure I know what gifted means because I've never been anything else.

Gifted, hmm, does that mean getting lots of presents?

Genius means little more than
perceiving in an unhabitual way.

— Henry James

THE PROBLEM WITH DEFINITIONS

I have one problem with this whole business of definitions. The problem isn't with the definitions themselves. It's with the *way* the definitions are *used*. Adults use them to develop criteria for identifying GTs who then receive special opportunities and more challenging educational programs.

That's fine. But no matter how hard teachers and administrators try, some gifted kids get left out. They aren't identified because they don't fit criteria set up by adults who do not, in fact, know precisely what a gifted kid should be like.

If you don't fit their description, if you don't conform, you miss out on the very opportunities that might enable you to demonstrate and enhance your giftedness.

Who Gets Left Out?

Those who are most often passed over when the gifted class Judgment Day comes along include:

Gifted Girls   May be eliminated not because they aren't as smart or as talented as boys, but because they may have learned to cover up or deny their abilities in order to be popular or feel "normal." After all, it's been only in the last few years that women have been encouraged to achieve.

The Handicapped   They may be excluded if their particular handicap hinders their ability to demonstrate giftedness in the most recognizable ways. The traditional methods used to identify GTs would never have identified a person like Helen Keller.

Troublemakers   They often aren't considered because some teachers (unfairly) associate good behavior with giftedness and bad behavior with — well, something other than giftedness. Thomas Edison, for example, was considered a little hellion in school. So much so that his teachers thought he was a real zero.

Culturally Different Students from culturally or racially different backgrounds get the short end from standard IQ and achievement tests. That's because these tests are often biased to the white, middle- to upper-class students in their use of terms and situations most familiar to them.

Lousy Test Takers Believe it or not, some GT students just aren't good at taking tests. Sure, they know the material but the test situation itself gets them uptight and as a consequence they do poorly. Sometimes they may be penalized by a bungling test administrator or personal problems. In situations like these, students are truly at a disadvantage because test scores are one of the principle methods used to identify GTs.

Borderline Cases Regardless of the system used to define and select gifted students, there are always those marginal cases who fall between the cracks. John F. Kennedy received constant reports of poor achievement and was a lousy speller. You can bet your booties he wouldn't have been selected for many GT classes.

What This Means To You

Simply this. Not everyone who is actually gifted has been identified as such. You may have friends, even brothers or sisters, who are gifted and have not been detected by the school's system for selection.

Some school's don't check for giftedness at all — so kids in those schools are *never* identified. Furthermore, if your test scores drop, *you* may be labeled "gifted" one year and not the next.

The System Is Not Perfect People Make Mistakes

The **important thing to remember is this: What *you* think of yourself and your abilities is foremost. Whether someone else tells you you're great or not is incidental. It is up to *you* to decide whether you will use your talents and abilities to the fullest — regardless of how exceptional they might be. It's up to you to see that you get what you want from life.**

As Paul, a 13-year-old GT put it,
"Not being able to use your talents, no matter what they are, is just like not having them."

Never, I mean *never* let anyone decide for you how smart you are. Be your own person. And remember:

**No one can make you feel inferior
without your consent.
— Anna Eleanor Roosevelt**

Here's a case in point. In the 1960s, Robert Rosenthal of Harvard and Lenore Jacobson, a teacher from San Francisco, used a classic experiment to demonstrate the power of expectations.

The researchers gave teachers some bogus information about students in their classes. The teachers were told that certain students were very bright and others were pretty dull. Can you guess what happened?

Right! The students who were *thought* to be bright did very well in school and those thought to be "slow" did not.

It wasn't the students' *inherent* abilities that caused them to do either very well or poorly. All of the students were actually intellectual equals. Rather, it was the teachers' expectations and encouragement that enabled students to do poorly or well.

The moral of the story is: when you believe in yourself, you can succeed. But if you're surrounded by a bunch of naysayers, success may be difficult if not impossible. As you read this book, then, be thinking about what you are now, what you want to become, and how you can help yourself to get there.

 "Whatever the cost in personal relationships, we discover that our highest responsibility, finally, unavoidably, is the stewardship of our potential — being all we can be."

— **Marilyn Ferguson**
The Aquarian Conspiracy

A Few GTs Who Made 'Em Eat Crow

Some of the world's greatest contributors have been misjudged by their teachers, their friends, even their parents. Take a look at some of the goofs committed against great minds of the past:

- Beethoven's music teacher once said of him, "As a composer, he is hopeless."
- Winston Churchill failed the 6th grade and finished last in his class at Harrow, England.
- Walt Disney was fired by a newspaper editor because "he had no good ideas."
- Louisa May Alcott was told by an editor that she could never write anything that had popular appeal.
- Gregor Mendel, founder of the science of genetics, flunked his teacher's examination four times and finally gave up trying to pass it.
- Charles Darwin, who originated the theory "Origin of the Species," quit medical school.
- Isaac Newton did poorly in grade school.

"it's okay kid —
I flunked math, too"

And even today, the minds of thousands of gifted students (we hope not yours) are being wasted. You might wonder how many Einsteins, Churchills and Alcotts are even today failing to survive a world that doesn't understand, much less educate them.

❖❖❖❖❖❖❖❖❖❖❖❖

And Now A Few Words From Teachers

❖❖❖❖❖❖❖❖❖❖❖❖

While it's easy to resent some of the things that go on in school these days, nobody can say that teachers and schools deliberately set out to shortchange GTs. Yet, it's human nature to point your finger and heap the blame on the person(s) closest at hand — teachers.

Some teachers deserve the criticism they get. Many more do not. They fall victim to a system which historically has been loaded with inequities. And while knowing where teachers are coming from won't solve your problems, it will help you to see both sides of the story.

• Right or wrong, most teachers aren't required to get training in gifted education. And even if they were, it's only been in the last 10 years that colleges have had classes on the subject. Therefore, many know very little about giftedness.

Fortunately, the situation is rapidly improving as more and more teacher colleges and universities begin to recognize the importance of gifted education.

• Authoritarian attitudes in our society are on the way out. From time immemorial teachers have ruled with an iron hand. Now, teachers and students are approaching a more democratic balance in making decisions in school. And it is your right to have it that way.

Still, many teachers resist change because they're not used to it. Old habits die hard.

• Tight school budgets mean fewer teachers and heavier workloads. And that means fewer opportunities to give GTs the individualized education they thrive on.

• Because more and more parents hold fulltime jobs, greater demands are placed on teachers. Things parents used to teach have become the responsibility of schools. Subjects like manners, health care and human sexuality, social skills and drug education...you name it. With more areas to cover, teachers have less time to spend with you. Less time to spend with every student.

The upshot of all this is that when you advocate for change in your school program, it can create additional problems for teachers. But the fact remains, your needs aren't "frills" but rather necessities. It is your right to request and receive a quality education suited to your learning abilities and needs.

How The Gifted Get Chosen

If you've got this book, it's likely you've already been selected for participation in a gifted program, but you may or may not know *how* you were selected.

Most times, teachers and school administrators rely on the following measures for selecting the gifted:

● **IQ Tests**

● **Achievement Tests**

● **Teacher Evaluations**

Some school districts ask for recommendations from parents or from students. And in a few instances, if you're really lucky, they might allow you to nominate yourself.

IQ

Say anything about intelligence and almost everybody thinks of IQ: Intelligence Quotient. Everybody's heard about it. And most everyone thinks IQ bears a one-to-one relationship with being GT. That is, if you have an average IQ, then you cannot possibly be GT. That's simply not true.

Still, because it is one of several measurements often used to determine giftedness, you ought to know a little more about it.

IQ tests came into use in the early 1900s, the work of psychologists Alfred Binet and Theodore Simon. They developed a test to identify, not kids who were gifted, but kids who were too dull to be educated in ordinary schools. (Only coincidentally did it measure gifted kids.) Later, another psychologist, Lewis Terman refined the Binet-Simon test to compare a person's mental age with his chronological age and thus the intelligence quotient was born.

Good or bad, IQ scores are frequently used to measure intellectual giftedness. And at one time, they were the *only* measure of giftedness.

Unfortunately, IQ scores, by themselves, mean very little. They don't measure creativity, leadership or communication ability. A high IQ does not guarantee success, higher grades, that you'll be president of your school class, captain of the track team or have the lead in the school play. They can't even predict whether you'll pass or fail.

What a high IQ does mean is that you have the *potential* to do well in *academics*. Potential unrealized is virtually useless.

There are many gifted people wasting away in prisons or working menial jobs because they haven't used their abilities in creative or productive ways.

The greatest minds are capable of the greatest vices as well as the greatest virtues.
— Rene Descartes, 1596-1650

Gerard Darrow, for example, was one of the brilliant Quiz Kids, GTs of the 1940s, who wowed radio and TV audiences with their smarts. He died at age 47, after spending a major portion of his final years on welfare and in poor health.

Willie Sidis, another child prodigy, graduated from high school by the time he was eight and lectured at Harvard when he was 11. In adulthood, Sidis became the target of much resentment by the press. He blamed his father for treating him as an exhibit and grew to reject intellectualism of any sort. He worked by choice at menial tasks and collected streetcar transfers as a hobby. He died at 46 in a rented room near Boston. His giftedness largely wasted, his brilliance so misunderstood.

And there are thousands of other examples, equally compelling. Just as there are millions of gifted students in the world wasting away in unchallenging school programs.

IQ scores are not the most important factor in determining whether you're GT or not. But they are important in defining *intellectual* giftedness and it's interesting to see how most people stack up.

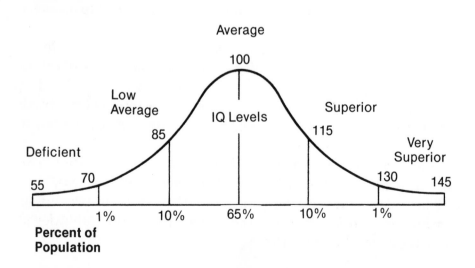

38

Now, take a look at the rarity of extraordinarily high IQs. When you see these numbers, it's easy to understand why many GTs feel alone in the world.

Number of people	out of	Have IQs of
3	100	130
1	100	137
1	1,000	150
1	10,000	160
1	100,000	168
1	1,000,000	180

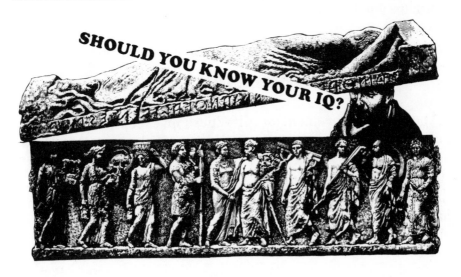

SHOULD YOU KNOW YOUR IQ?

Most teachers and parents aren't particularly keen about sharing IQ scores with students. They fear you'll use the information in all the wrong ways.

For example, if someone said you've got the IQ of a mental midget, you'd most likely get down on yourself and do poorly in school.

Conversely, if you found out that your IQ was close to Einstein's, you might start bragging, stop working and flunk out.

There are others who believe that providing IQ scores is beneficial. They say some students are more motivated when they learn their IQs. It boosts their self-esteem. What do you think?

But...

If you *really* want to know your IQ, ask your school counselor or parents. If they won't tell you, test yourself using IQ tests available at bookstores. Two I found were: *Self-Scoring IQ Test* by Alfred W. Munzert or *How Intelligent Are You?* by Victor Serebriakoff. They're kind of fun to do and they might give you an idea of where you're at. But remember, when you get your answer, be cool. Use the information wisely.

Achievement Tests

Another measurement of giftedness or exceptional talent is taken from achievement tests. You've no doubt taken these tests many times. Remember: "Fill in the spaces with number 2 pencil lead and don't turn to the next page until you're told." Obviously, if you do exceedingly well on these tests, it shows that you're learning what you're supposed to be learning in school. It also indicates that you're a good test taker.

Teacher Evaluations

Still another measurement comes from teachers themselves. These are very subjective guidelines, in which the teacher gives his or her gut reaction about which students show exceptional abilities in various areas. Here's a sample of one:

Teacher Screening Form

Gifted Education

Will you please take a few minutes to write in the first and last names
of the children whose names come into your mind first as you look at
the terms below? This should be done as free association, very rapidly.
You need not fill in every space, and to save time, if you list a child
more than once, use the first name and last initial to save time after
the first listing. Thank you very much.

1. Learns easily, quickly _____

2. Original, imaginative, creative, unconventional _____

3. Widely informed, wide interests beyond chronological age _____

4. Persistent, resourceful, self-directed _____

5. Common sense, may not tolerate foolishness _____

6. Inquisitive, skeptical _____

7. Informed in unusual areas _____

8. Artistic _____

9. Outstanding vocabulary, verbally fluent _____

10. Musical _____

11. Independent worker, shows initiative _____

12. Good judgement, logical _____

13. Flexible, open _____

14. Versatile, many interests _____

15. Shows unusual insights _____

16. Shows high level of sensitivity, empathy toward others _____

17. Has excellent sense of humor _____

18. Resists routine and drill _____

19. Expresses ideas and reactions, sometimes in an argumentative way

_____

20. Sensitive to truth and honor _____

In addition to teacher evaluations, there are student questionnaires which normally follow a similar format. To see how you stack up, go down the list on the previous page and check the characteristics that best describe you.

What these evaluations attempt to do is identify GTs from several categories of ability. Obviously, no one, no matter how gifted, is going to exhibit *all* of the traits mentioned. Certainly a gifted mathematician will show different abilities than a great dancer. So we've regrouped the characteristics to show how giftedness is demonstrated in five areas.

Academic Ability
High rate of success in subjects of interest
Pursues certain areas with vigor
Good memory
Comprehends well
Acquires knowledge quickly
Widely read in special areas

Intellectual
Observant
Gets excited about
  new ideas
Inquisitive
Learns rapidly, easily
Independent learner
Has a large vocabulary
  compared to others of same age
Thinks abstractly
Enjoys Hypothesizing
Intense

Leadership
Likes structure
Self-confident
Well-accepted by peers
Shows good judgment, common sense
Responsible
Articulate, verbally fluent
Foresees the consequences of things

Creative
Independent thinker
Expressive (oral or written)
Keen sense of humor
Is resourceful
Doesn't mind being different
Is original, unconventional, imaginative

Visual/Performing Arts
Ability for expressing feelings, thoughts and
  moods through art, dance, drama or music
Good coordination
Exhibits creativity, imagination
Observant
Likes to produce original products
Flexible

How You Get Gifted

Most students don't know they're gifted until somebody comes along and tells them so. They know they're different from others, but aren't sure why or how.

Usually, the someone that gives you the good news is a teacher or a counselor. They report results from tests you've taken which show you're smarter or more creative than average. Now that you know you're GT, and you have at least a passing idea of what being gifted is all about, you're probably asking yourself: How did I get this way?

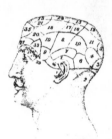 # Where Giftedness
Comes From

It may come as a surprise to you but intelligence or talent is, in part, inherited.

Quite simply put, your mom or dad (and quite possibly both) are GT too. Or maybe you inherited your giftedness from somewhere deeper in the family chain—perhaps a grandmother or grandfather.

The other factor that determines your level of GT ability is environment. **Everything** around you—your experiences with friends, family and at school, books you've read, games you play, everything in your environment contributes to the enhancement of gifted abilities.

While no one knows exactly which of these factors is most important in determining GT ability, we **do** know that there are things you can do to maximize (and likewise minimize), your giftedness.

Things like being active, reading a lot, meeting new people, traveling, being inquisitive and taking advantage of life's opportunities—all of these things help you to become more knowledgeable and creative. They give you the opportunity to stretcccccchhhhh your mind and grow as a person.

And it works both ways. If you lead a boring life, watch the tube all day long, avoid books like the plague and do your best to stop stimulation, you're going to put the old IQ on hold. You may even lower it. It has been shown that IQs can vary as much as 20 points throughout a person's life. Everyone experiences mental as well as physical growth spurts and plateaus.

How Many Are Gifted?

Today, it is estimated that there are between two and three million gifted kids in the U.S. alone. If you live outside the United States, you can figure about five percent of the population using common definitions and selection practices.

Naturally, not everyone agrees with those numbers. A few educators suggest that if we broaden definitions enough, as many as 60 percent of the population could be defined as gifted. There are even some who believe that *everyone* is GT in some way.

Regardless of how we define GT, and whether you come up with a gifted population of five or fifty percent, one thing is for certain: school can be a headache for GTs.

SCHOOL SURVIVAL 101

*"Genius without education is
like silver in the mine."*

— Ben Franklin 1706-1790

*"Going to school is about as
exciting as watching grass grow."*

Ask GTs about school and most will be quick to say that it's their #1 hassle in life.

It's boring.
It's too easy.
It's repetitious.
It's irrelevant.
It's blah, blah, blah.

And the reason schoolwork is too easy, too repetitive, too mundane, too trivial, and too blah is because it doesn't match your intellectual interests and capabilities. It matches *someone else's* interests and capabilities.

So who is school for?

Well, in some respects, it's built for all of us. Schools teach us, in simple terms, how to get along in this world: how to read, write, speak, and act so we can be responsible citizens.

We take courses like history, civics, math, chemistry, foreign languages, English I and II, Home Ec, etc. And that's about it.

The list of courses hasn't changed much since your father and mother went to school. And their parents. And perhaps that's as it should be. We do, in fact, need the basics. Schools do a pretty good job of teaching average kids average stuff.

Another reason schools are into average is "cost efficiency." Or more simply put, getting the most out of their money.

Schools have to be cost effective because they just don't have enough money to do everything. They never had it. They never will.

As a result, there isn't a lot of room for creativity — or so some people think. Students who need special education often get lost in the shuffle. And that includes slow learners and gifted kids as well.

Worse yet, some school systems actually develop anti-intellectual attitudes. In some communities, if you're not into athletics, you might as well exit stage left. And as a result, those who enjoy learning and mind stimulating pursuits get ridiculed or ignored instead of helped.

Nobody knows better than GTs what's wrong with that whole scene. You simply want an education that fits the way your mind works. Nothing militant, mind you — you just want to:

 Learn at your own speed, not some-one else's

 Skip over work you already know and understand

 Study things of interest beyond basic schoolwork

 Work with abstract concepts that require more than simple thinking — creative, reflective, analytical ideas, for example.

When you don't get an opportunity to stretch your mind in at least *some* of these ways, you get bored. And when you get bored, you may bail out.

In 1972, the U.S. Office of Education reported that many gifted and talented students drop out of school before graduation. Some of the reasons they bailed out included a dislike for school and a desire to get a job instead. A job seemed more meaningful.

Small wonder. Kids are wise about what's right and wrong in their lives:

> *"Smart children soon learn that what is important in school is one thing — and what is important in life is another, and they live in this schizophrenic existence satisfactorily. Many, however, do not. Everything we learn doesn't have to be relevant. But if some of our school learning isn't meaningful, we may get turned off enough so that we don't want to learn anything anywhere. We may simply drop out."*
> — **William Glasser**
> ***Schools Without Failure***

And there's the rub. Can you survive school if you find it irrelevant and boring?

Sure you can. It may be dullsville, but you can survive. But what if you want to do *more* than survive? What if you actually want to learn a lot in school?

A BREATH OF FRESH AIR

If you're bummed out about school, remember, it doesn't have to be boring and irrelevant. Today, teachers all over the world are designing programs to meet the needs of gifted and talented students. We need to give credit where credit is due. Some teachers have challenged and respected students from day one. We're sure you've had teachers like this. They:

Are flexible

Have a good sense of humor

Don't expect perfection

Are willing to help

Make learning fun and don't stick to the textbook

Understand the pluses and minuses
of giftedness

Are inspiring

Don't pretend to know everything

If you're fortunate, you know at least one terrific teacher. And perhaps you're in classes that interest and challenge you. But if you're not so lucky, or if you'd like to see even more happening for GTs, knowing what *can* be done will help you on the road to making changes — in your favor.

We'll give you some ideas for altering your school program to tailor it for *your* needs, *your* abilities, *your* learning style, *your* interests. Things can change — but not unless you take some of the responsibility for it. Other GTs have done it. So can you.

"Genius is one percent inspiration and ninety-nine percent perspiration."

— Thomas Edison

Seven Steps For Getting More GT Education In Your School

1. Take your own inventory. Decide what you need that your school isn't providing.

2. Check the menu for GT entrees.

3. Is your school with it? Or without it?

4. Get your head together.

5. Make a plan.

6. Find the Movers and Shakers.

7. Do it — stop procrastinating.

Step One: Taking your own inventory

To help you figure out what's right and wrong with your classes, ask yourself:

- Is work in every class too easy?
- Is one specific subject too easy? (Math or science or English or what?)
- Do you have a special interest which isn't taught by any teachers? (i.e. astronomy, paleontology or Russian)
- Have you taken all the required courses and you're only a sophomore?
- Are you planning to go to college? Do you want a head start?
- Do you find you need more uninterrupted time when working on projects? One period just isn't enough.
- Do you wish there were more GTs in your class?
- Are you kind of satisfied with regular classes but wish they could be expanded to include higher level thinking?
- Do you want to work independently more often?
- Is there a person in the community you'd like to learn from?

As you go on to Step Two, be thinking about which programs will meet your needs. And don't be limited to our list. Be creative! Dream up your own idea if none of these programs suit you.

Step Two — Today's menu for GTs

ACCELERATION

Commonly known as skipping a grade, acceleration allows you to jump to a higher level of classwork than your age would ordinarily dictate.

The jump can either be for a particular class, or you can skip an entire grade.

Acceleration is usually considered when you can work at a level, usually two or more years, beyond other kids your age.

While acceleration is reasonably commonplace, many adults have historically been against it. They worry that if you start rubbing elbows with kids older than you, "you'll suffer emotionally." And yet there isn't a single study which shows that acceleration has, in fact, caused any great problems for anybody.

On the contrary, many studies show that when you're allowed to learn at your own pace, you feel better about yourself, are more motivated and creative, have greater aspirations, and are more socially "with it." Who could ask for more?

COLLEGE ENROLLMENT

Typically, gifted students finish school requirements before their senior year.

If the high school they attend cannot teach specialized courses that students need or want, the result of limited enrollment, budget cuts or unqualified staff, they're left with no place to go except college.

Some school districts allow high school students to either graduate early or enroll in college courses while finishing out their high school years.

BACK-TO-BACK CLASSES

Here's a clever way to get an extra-long class period by pairing classes.

In this arrangement, two classes are scheduled one right after another. For example, social studies and language arts.

By scheduling classes this way, teachers and kids have more opportunities to do things that require more time than an hour-long class can provide (how many times have you just gotten started with an exciting project only to have the bell ring right in the middle of it?).

Back-to-back classes also make it easier for teachers to use a variety of learning and teaching styles like independent study, debate, drama, field trips or extended discussions.

ENRICHMENT

School enrichment programs are designed to replace, or extend the regular school curriculum.

The goal of enrichment should be to help you work on high level skills; such as divergent and evaluative thinking, problem-solving and creativity. Some of the ways these skills can be taught are through debates and discussions, research or simulations.

A program in Mullica Hill, New Jersey is a good example of this sort of in-school enrichment program. GT students have one semester of enrichment and one semester of independent study. Said Brett, 13, "In this class, we mainly do things that we don't do in the regular subjects. It's fun and it makes you think. But not everybody could hack it. Some kids just couldn't do the work."

RESOURCE ROOMS

Resource rooms can be havens for the gifted, where they can make new friends of similar intellect, work on fascinating projects and use special equipment.

Usually, the teacher who works in these special resource rooms is sensitive to the needs of the GT and is not threatened by students who quite often know more than they do about certain things.

If you want to work in an atmosphere where you're free to use your talents and abilities without criticism from others, a resource room could be your salvation.

MENTORSHIPS

Mentorships enable gifted students to be paired with an adult or student who is an expert in a particular study or profession they'd like to pursue. Mentors come from either the academic or business community.

Usually, students and mentors agree to work together closely for a set period of time. Meetings are arranged during or after school hours as determined by the participants.

Accelerated and enriched learning are the natural consequences of mentorships. Mentorships also provide good career exploration opportunities.

In Minneapolis, Minnesota, a program known as The Mentor Connection offers mentorships for students all year long. Before being placed with a mentor, students participate in a guidance lab to learn advanced research skills, decision making, self-awareness and career awareness. Participants of The Mentor Connection had this to say about their experiences:

> *"I gained a broader horizon of insight in human experience. The diversity of people who worked at my site is staggering. Trying to meet and get along with all these new people was very exciting."*
> **Randy, 17**
> Placed in research and design,
> Control Data Corporation

> *"I was very pleased with my mentor; we related very well to each other. The people at the YWCA accepted me with open arms. The most beneficial part of the experience was getting out into the working world and finding out what it's really like."*
> **Paula, 18**
> Placed at the YWCA

INDEPENDENT STUDY

When you want to "do your own thing," an independent study may be just the ticket.

Such a program allows you to work at your own pace in a program of your special interest. A mentor or teacher serves as a guide. Then you're on your own — sink or swim.

Most independent study programs require you to:
- Develop a plan stating the subject of the study
- List your goals, objectives
- Plan activities to achieve your goals
- Complete a final product

Study plans often take the form of a contract.

GTs from Windsor, Colorado, participate in an independent study program called ALP, Autonomous Learning Process. They contract for projects throughout the school year and meet regularly in small groups. Above all, this program is what it says it is — Independent.

"The main thing this program has taught me is how to kick myself in the rear. In a normal classroom, the teacher hangs over you ready to cut your head off if you don't do the assignments. In ALPs, you get a project and it's up to you to get it done. I think it's important to learn to be responsible for yourself."

Charles, 17

"For me, the best part of this program is being able to do your own thing. I do about three major studies each year — all things I wouldn't have the opportunity to study in regular classes. It really challenges you to accomplish more."

Greg, 15

FIELD TRIPS AND CULTURAL EVENTS

Everybody benefits from field trips and cultural events, especially GTs. Why? Because they perceive things more deeply. They're more inquisitive — they ask more questions. GTs want to know how things work.

Trips to the zoo, the symphony, a museum, a bakery, banks or a sewage plant will broaden your horizons. Where would you like to visit?

ADVANCED PLACEMENT

Advanced Placement (AP) classes are just super for students who are looking for greater academic challenge, more opportunities for accomplishment and individual progress.

Students in AP classes take college-level courses taught by highly qualified high school teachers right on their own high school campus. AP classes may take the form of an honors class, a strong regular class or an independent study. If you successfully complete the courses, you receive either high school credit, advance standing college credit, or advanced college placement by taking and passing an AP exam. Best of all, AP allows you to avoid repeating work you've already done.

Over 5,000 high schools in the U.S. have AP programs. Your principal, teachers, or counselors should be able to tell you about AP — whether your school has such classes or could start them.

And can you learn? Just listen!

"I was just learning facts and more facts. [The AP teacher] taught us the tools and techniques of scholarship so you could see what facts you need to know and how to get them."

*

"I liked working with kids of my ability or even more ability and maybe it's because it makes me work harder."

*

"I fought my way in — went to the teacher, the principal, everybody. I was tired of learning nothing and wasting time in classes with kids who didn't care about anything but being 16 and getting out of school."

For further information about AP, write to:
Advanced Placement Program
45 Columbus Avenue
New York, NY 10023

SEMINARS AND MINI-COURSES

These classes, now becoming quite commonplace, are for students, gifted or not, with similar interests and abilities. There's nothing new about recognizing that people with common interests support each other and make learning more fun.

Classes may be offered during or after school, or on weekends. Usually, they're taught by teachers or members of the community.

SUMMER SCHOOL

Summer school programs vary greatly from school to school. When budgets are tight, some schools eliminate summer school altogether. But when schools have the bucks, they may offer a variety of classes designed to challenge GTs.

In Hopkins, seven Minnesota school districts pooled their resources to offer summer school programs for GTs. The West Suburban Summer School, as it's been named, provides more than 35 courses each summer. One 10th grader, in demonstrating her support of the school, told me:

"The hardest part for me is making a decision about which class to take — there's such a variety."

Another added:

"It was fun *and* challenging."

A parent wrote and said, "A true test (of the school's success) was that our son was willing to get up and go that early on a summer morning."

How Does Your School Measure Up?

The next step is to determine if your school has any of the programs we mentioned (sometimes options are kept secret only because no one asks.) Or, are they contemplating starting one? If they are, you won't have to start planning from scratch.

There are two or three places you can go to find out. If the program involves a specific academic area, for example, go to the teacher who teaches that subject or a department head.

Perhaps you may wish to see about being accelerated in English. Simple. Ask your English teacher if the school allows for such changes.

Or suppose you want to establish a new class on computer programming. Maybe a science teacher can tell you if the school is contemplating such a program.

You might also check with your high school counselor. Believe it or not, however, most gifted kids don't deal a lot with counselors. Yet counselors are there to help you as much as any other student.

The final step, if you still haven't answered your question, is to go straight to the horse's mouth — the principal. Make an appointment to see him or her if necessary and get the answers to your questions.

Know The Requirements

If your school has requirements for participation in a program that you want to join, find out what they are. If you don't qualify, see what you can do to change your status. If the requirements seem ridiculous or unfair — list your reasons for feeling that way and share them with the person in charge.

Request admission on probation if necessary. If, after a reasonable time, you don't work well in the class or program, be prepared to drop out and move on to something which is right for you.

If your school is without . . .

If after careful searching, you find that there aren't any programs offered which will meet your needs, go directly to Step 4.

Getting Your Head Together
Preparing For Change

It's one thing to *know* what you'd like to have changed about your school program and quite another to *do something* about it, to improve your lot.

Throughout life, we all face obstacles in carrying out our business. It's inevitable. But how we *perceive* those obstacles is paramount to the question of whether we solve them or not.

Some people, for example, simply cop out of a difficult situation. It's just too much for them to manage, or so they think. And if they *perceive* a problem as being too difficult, it will be. Whether it *is*, in fact, too much to handle is academic because they've given up before finding out.

Other people look at problems as a challenge. They do not recite all the reasons why something *can't* be done. They start looking for ways why something *can* be done. Then they do it.

Set Goals

Without exception, the students who get the most out of school told me they SET GOALS. Not only were they excellent goal-setters, they spent a good deal of time figuring out *how* these goals would be accomplished. (See our section on the "how-to's" of goal setting.)

Taking Risks

There are several obstacles which may prevent you from making changes in your school program — chief among these is your own motivation.

Mike, a high school student, has been very successful in switching things around at his school. He summed it up very nicely:

"I think a lack of assertiveness can prevent kids from asking for changes in school. There are those who simply put their fate in the hands of others and trust that everything will come out right. They just don't push.

"Another thing I see is kids who aren't willing to accept that the school could make a mistake. They believe the school always knows best. I even know some kids who are afraid to change things for fear they'll hurt the teacher's feelings by dropping out of their class and taking something else. In that situation kids just live a lie. Everybody loses."

On Winning

Anytime we try to improve our lives, we must accept the fact that sometimes we'll win and sometimes we'll lose. That's the way life really is.

But remember that life is constantly changing. You may not succeed now but perhaps you'll succeed in the future.

You may have to wait until you are older, or have more money, or have more clout or more time. Any number of factors affect how our lives will turn out.

Meanwhile, do what you can to make your life as good as it can be. And don't wait. Do it now!

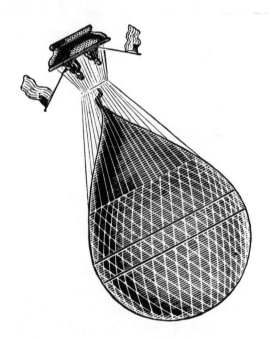

Question Authority

Changes of any sort are rarely made unless somebody is willing to step forward, challenge authority and question the system.

School changes are not any different.

That means recognizing and accepting that adults make mistakes — teachers make mistakes (and you make mistakes). Contrary to what they may tell you, adults do not always have the best answers.

It also means that you'll have to take *risks*. And just as you'll have something to gain, you'll have something to lose. The loss usually takes the form of resentment by a teacher for "rocking the boat." Or they may feel threatened by your request and become defensive. But whatever. In order to get what you want out of life, you have to be willing to take the risk.

So right here and now, give yourself permission to question authority. It's your right and your responsibility — that is, if you're running your own life.

Commit Yourself And Be Prepared To Work

As mentioned earlier, change is never easy, no matter who is involved. As a result, you must be prepared to commit your heart, body, and soul to your dreams and goals. Without commitment, you may not be strong enough to do what needs to be done in order to get what you want.

> *We must remind ourselves, however, that no change takes place without working hard and without getting our hands dirty. There are no formulae and no books to memorize on becoming. I only know this: I exist, I am, I am here, I am becoming. I make my life and no one else makes it for me. I must face my own shortcomings, mistakes, transgressions. No one can suffer my non-being as I do, but tomorrow is another day, and I must decide to leave my bed and live again. And if I fail, I don't have the comfort of blaming you or life or God.*
>
> **Joseph Zinker,**
> **Gestalt Institute of Cleveland**

Most people do not plan to fail.
They simply fail to plan.

Make A Plan

Making a plan is nothing more than doing homework for the movers and shakers of your school. It's a way of making their job easier. Of proving that you've carefully thought about the problem, possible solutions, and that above all, you're serious about it.

For example, if you're unsatisfied with a class and would like to propose a new one especially for GTs, you should be able to answer as many of these questions as possible:

What's the subject area? Be as specific as you can.
When and where will it meet?
Do you know how many other students might want to take this course?
What are the qualifications for entry?
Who will teach it?
Will it cost money? Save money?
Do you want to receive credit for the class?
What are some problems that may be encountered?
Why is this class valuable?
What will this class replace?

These are the sorts of questions that movers and shakers will be asking . . . questions that you have to be prepared to help answer.

Obviously, your proposal will make a lot more sense to you, as well as the movers and shakers, if you get your plan down on paper.

You must identify the man or woman who has the power to put into effect the change you desire.

Finding the Movers and Shakers

In the hierarchy of any school system there are individuals who have the power to make change. The person might be the principal. She might be head of a department. He might be a teacher. He or she might be the superintendent of schools. The point is, you are going to have to find the person who can help you make change and the only way to find out is to ask.

Bring your plan to a person who may be directly involved. For example, if you want to start an accelerated math class, go to a person in the math department. Find out if she supports your plan and if she has the power to help you get the ball rolling. If not, move on to someone who does.

CAUTION:

Don't be discouraged if the person you approach neither likes your program nor is willing to support it. He may have an ax to grind. He may have to teach the class and regards it simply as more work. He may think your plan is dumb — and he could be dead wrong! Just remember, teachers aren't perfect. Nobody's perfect.

Getting Help

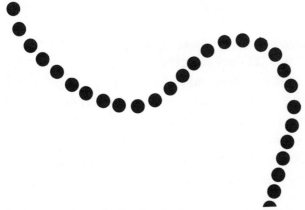

You may need all the help you can get to find and influence the movers and shakers. Don't walk — run to solicit the support of people who can help. That may mean a parent, the local PTA, your school board, a counselor, other GTs, the Student Council or a gifted education advocacy group.

You might have to do some things you don't want to do, like attend a PTA or school board meeting. But it's a small price to pay in order to get what you want.

Remember that while there are some adults who are insensitive, sarcastic, boring or disrespectful of kids, there are also many who aren't that way. Our advice is to surround yourself with as many of the broad-minded and supportive ones you can find. It'll make working with the uncooperative ones more tolerable.

7

Now comes the time to do it and stop procrastinating

Here's the part that's easier said than done . . . getting off your duff and putting your plan into action. Just remember the earlier quote of the 16-year-old who said of his AP class, "I fought my way in — went to the teacher, the principal, everybody." That's the kind of motivation and commitment you'll need to get your program off and flying.

"You gain strength, courage and confidence by every experience in which you really stop to look fear in the face. You are able to say to yourself, I lived through this horror. I can take the next thing that comes along . . . You must do the thing you think you cannot do."

Anna Eleanor Roosevelt

In the Meantime . . .
SIX THINGS GTS DO (IN CLASS) WHEN THEY'RE BORED

"When we're going over something (in class) for the zillionth time, at first I try to listen. That doesn't last long though — then I let my mind wander. Daydreaming helps."

Derek, 14

*

"When I'm done with school work (and even sometimes when I'm not), I read to make things more interesting. I figure I learn more by reading than by doing most of the assignments we're given. I try to go to the public library as often as I can because our school's library doesn't have as much. Books are my salvation."

Bill, 16

*

"When things get boring in school, I try to get more involved. That makes me feel better."

Jan, 15

*

"I have to be really interested in a subject or else I get bored. When a class is boring, I try to make a challenge out of it or the assignments just to get me through, just to get it done and out of the way so I can go on to other things that are more interesting."

Lynn, 15

*

"When I'm bored in school, I read over my notes to make sure I get an A on the test. If I've done that, I do extra credit. I make goals for myself to see how much I can get done. I write them down so I can keep track of how I'm doing and I usually meet or exceed my expectations. Usually school work is too easy though and I think it should be harder."

Robert, 13

*

"When I get an assignment that requires me to do things I've already learned, I ask certain teachers if I can do something else. It helps if I have something specific in mind so they don't think I'm just going to slough off. Most of the time they don't object. There are a few teachers who would get mad if I ever asked to do something different though."

Mary, 14

As Mary noted above, some teachers can be bad news when it comes to making changes.

But before you indict all teachers, give a listen to their side:

"Teaching school can get boring and sometimes I feel as though I have to be a superstar to get them turned on. If a student approaches me in a non-threatening and helpful way, I appreciate hearing ideas about how things can be made more interesting. It takes some of the burden off me. I'm human. I don't react very well to a verbal attack about how boring school is. Especially when the person hasn't got any ideas of his own."

In other words, rather than accusing a teacher of being boring, unfair, stupid, inflexible, or some other uncomplimentary adjective (even if it's the truth) you'll likely get what you want if you ask for a teacher's *help*. Turn things around so that the odds will be in your favor.

For example, if you want to test out of the regular assignments because you already know the material and would rather work on an independent project, see which of these approaches would get the most favorable response:

Dialog A

Student: Mr. or Ms. Jones, I have a concern that I'd like to talk with you about. It has to do with our vocabulary assignment.

Teacher: Yes, what's the problem?

Student: Well, each week on Monday we get the assignment for learning 30 new vocabulary words. Friday, after doing all of the textbook assignments and worksheets, we take a test to show that we've learned the words. Most of the time, as you can see by my grades, I get A's on the tests. But I could get A's even without doing all of the assignments. I guess I know a lot of vocabulary because I read so much or something. Anyway, I was wondering if I could take

70

the vocabulary test at the beginning of the week and if I passed, say with 95 percent correct, if I could work on some other projects instead of doing the assignments the other kids do to learn words? I feel my time would be better spent learning some new things. Would you be willing to at least try it out for a few weeks? Here is one project I would like to do.

Dialog B

Student: Mr. or Ms. Smith, I have to tell you that I think your class really stinks. It's so boring. I never learn anything here. I don't think I should have to do any of these dumb assignments either.

Teacher: (In self defense) Well, that's too bad. You're no better than anyone else here and the assignment stands. And seeing as you're so bored and you want to get an A in this class, you can do 100 points of extra credit.

It's pretty obvious that dialog A will be more likely to get favorable results.

Finesse is everything when dealing with people. Don't make things worse for yourself by being antagonistic. (This may be preachy, but it is also true.)

And one last tip; this one from Tim, 14:

> "You get a better response from teachers if you talk with them *before* or *after* school. Trying to get help in between classes is useless — there just isn't time. Asking a teacher to help you in some way (especially if what you're doing requires that they make an exception to the rule) is best done when other people aren't around. By talking to the teacher privately, you don't put them in an awkward position in front of other kids."

DESIDERATA

Go placidly amid the noise and haste, and remember what peace there may be in silence. As far as possible without surrender be on good terms with all persons. Speak your truth quietly and clearly; and listen to others, even the dull and ignorant; they too have their story.

Avoid loud and aggressive persons, they are vexatious to the spirit. If you compare yourself with others, you may become vain and bitter; for always there will be greater and lesser persons than yourself. Enjoy your achievements as well as your plans.

Keep interested in your own career, however humble; it is a real possession in the changing fortunes of time. Exercise caution in your business affairs; for the world is full of trickery. But let this not blind you to what virtue there is; many persons strive for high ideals; and everywhere life is full of heroism.

Be yourself. Especially, do not feign affection. Neither be cynical about love; for in the face of all aridity and disenchantment it is perennial as the grass.

Take kindly the counsel of the years, gracefully surrendering the things of youth. Nurture strength of spirit to shield you in sudden misfortune. But do not distress yourself with imaginings. Many fears are born of fatigue and loneliness. Beyond a wholesome discipline, be gentle with yourself.

You are a child of the universe, no less than the trees and the stars, you have a right to be here. And whether or not it is clear to you, no doubt the universe is unfolding as it should. Therefore, be at peace with God, whatever you conceive Him to be, and whatever your labors and aspirations, in the noisy confusion of life keep peace with your soul.

With all its sham, drudgery and broken dreams, it is still a beautiful world. Be cheerful. Strive to be happy.

— Max Ehrmann

A Few Words About Being Perfect

One of the most troubling aspects about being gifted is that many times, people expect you not only to be *good* at *everything* you do — but they expect perfection.

What's worse is many GTs start believing that baloney. They start thinking that these people are right, they should be perfect.

"Sometimes, when a friend asks me a question and I can't answer it, I feel like I've let him down."

Paul, 13

"My parents have very high expectations of me. I try to fulfill them but sometimes I fall flat on my face. When that happens, sometimes they just forget it but other times 30 minutes of yelling follows. First I feel guilty. Then I get mad at myself and later, I feel angry at them for having such high expectations of me. It's a lot of pressure. I'm more relaxed with myself than they are with me."

Derek, 14

"Sometimes, I wish I was less intelligent so I could accept defeat better. I always think, I'm so intelligent. Therefore, I should be getting an A no matter what the subject is."

Missy, 17

"Teachers, not very many, but a few, will try to make you look bad by asking you questions that they know you don't know the answers to. It's humiliating."

Rob, 14

"If I bring home a report card with all A's and one A-, you know which grade I hear about? The A-."

Jim, 15

"I worry about getting good grades a lot. Some teachers judge tests by how I do on them. If I get everything right, they figure the test was too easy. If I get a C or something, they figure the test was too hard. I feel bad if I get a C. When that happens they (the teachers) sometimes bring the grading curve down. It's a lot of pressure.

John, 13

73

Now I ask you, do these comments sound familiar? And does this sound like a rational way to live?

Absolutely not!

Nothing could be more irrational than insisting on perfect performance day in and day out and then getting down on yourself when you can't measure up to this unobtainable goal. And most of the time, it is the adults who keep insisting that perfectionism is the way to go: that doing it your way is wrong.

Well, for once (at least) in your life, YOU ARE ABSOLUTELY RIGHT. It's the rest of the world that is wrong. All wrong. And feel free to confront your parents, your teachers, your friends, or anyone else who tries to tell you otherwise.

It's absolutely stupid to try to be perfect. It's just as dumb to be told to at least "always give it your best shot."

First of all, we can't be perfect. Michelangelo was a pretty fair painter, for example, but his math was shabby by comparison. You may be super at math, and lousy in art. Or you may be super at math *some* of the time, but only "quite good" or even average at other times.

And the same can be said for "giving it your best shot" all the time. "All we ask is that you do your best," comes the admonition. To which you might reply: "Baloney."

Certainly, there are some impressive benefits from doing things well. Studying hard and achieving top grades may mean a lot of things: approval from teachers and parents, special privileges, (especially from your parents), more challenging opportunities, and the like. And if that sort of thing makes you happy (and I don't know why it shouldn't), it's a pretty good deal.

But really, to do your best *all the time?* Does your father do his best *all the time* when he goes to his job? Does your mother? Absolutely not. Sometimes they have off days, and perform at levels something less than their best. It's passable. But not their best. Sometimes, they do the most important part of their work the best they can, and leave other portions of their work, just so-so.

And you can do the same thing. Pick and choose areas you really want to be great in and do the rest however you want.

Thus, it may be *desirable* to get straight A's, but you can live with 4 A's and a B. It might be nice to be captain of the tennis team *and* the #1 player, but even lousy tennis players like me have plenty of fun simply playing the game — rather than playing it *perfectly.*

It's a no-win situation when you do only things at which you are exceptional — merely because you feel you've got to please somebody. If you buckle under the fear of pressure and attempt only what you're good at, you'll miss out on a lot of life.

Moreover, you do not become a "better person" even if you do many things more successfully than others. Getting straight A's in math, for example, might bring all sorts of approvals from teachers, family and friends, but it doesn't make you a better person — only smarter in math. And that's hardly comparable to being a "nicer person."

So what do you tell a parent or a teacher who gets on your case for not getting top grades *all* the time, in *all* your classes? What do you tell *yourself* when you start getting the guilties?

LEVELING

1. First of all, level with yourself. You may or may not be disappointed with a lower grade. You may be angry at yourself. And if you are angry or disappointed, why do you feel that way? Was the grade undeserved? Did you have an "off day?" Are you simply disinterested in the subject and are saving your mental energy for higher grades in some other course?

When you understand the reasons for your performance, you can level with whoever is getting on your case. It takes guts but it can and must be done if you want to get people to quit hassling you.

2. If it's a teacher, s/he may be concerned with your performance because it reflects on their performance. If you had an off day or aren't interested in the class or subject, assure the teacher your grades have nothing to do with their teaching — you simply aren't interested in the subject and don't want to put forth A-work effort.

3. To a parent or teacher, you might say, "I realize I didn't do as well as I might have on (the subject, the test, the project, etc.) but I do very well on *most* of my work and that's good enough for me.

4. Is there a reason why I *should* be doing better on this subject, class, test, etc? Is it needed to make the honor roll? Is it a prerequisite for another class?

5. Parents, after they become accustomed to your routine of bringing home high grades, often focus more attention on the occasional lower grade than your overall success.

Take the case of Ann B. who quite regularly brought home straight A's and then came home with four A's and one B. As happens all too often with GTs, her father asked, "What happened in English? I thought English was easy for you." rather than "Gee, four A's. That's terrific and I'm glad you enjoy doing well in school, Ann."

You might explain that you're having to do a lot more work to get good grades and that you were able to get 4 A's *because* you took the B in English. That you just don't have enough study time to get all A's.

6. Perhaps there *is* a reason why you might want to do better in that subject. And maybe there isn't. If it's just top grades for the sake of top grades, with no concrete reason, you have less incentive to work harder. If you have specific reasons for wanting great grades, for example, to qualify for a top college, because you learn more when you work harder or to get a scholarship, you're more likely to achieve the goal.

7. You might want to level about why you took the course in the first place. "I only took the course because (1) I thought it would be fun and the grade isn't important; (2) This course isn't very important, interesting or whatever, but I need it to graduate. (3) The class was a prerequisite for another course I want to take.

With a little practice, you can begin to put these ill-advised notions about perfectionism in proper perspective. Obviously, not only do you have to get your own thinking in order about being perfect, you also have to set the record straight with others. So go ahead, take a subject you *enjoy* rather than one you excel at. It may not raise your GPA or score points with your parents, but it may do wonders for your motivation in school. And after all, you spend a great deal of time there — shouldn't some of it be just for you?

Happiness can be found in simply *doing*, not only in doing things well.

What is a friend?
It is another I.

Zeno, 335-263 B.C.

FRIENDS

I don't think anyone can argue about the importance of having friends. They support us in good times and bad. They enhance the joy of doing many things: football games, parties, dances, and more. We all need them, and being gifted or talented doesn't have anything to do with it.

GTs — like all kids — sometimes have problems dealing with and making friends. But many times, the problems GTs face are the *direct result* of being gifted.

Ten Common Concerns
GTs Have About Their Friends:

1. I have trouble getting them to understand me.

2. It's hard to get along with kids my own age.

3. I hate being labeled "gifted" by kids. It makes me feel too different.

4. I hate being teased about being smart.

5. Kids tease me when I *don't get* A's all the time.

6. Kids tease me when I *get* A's all the time.

7. My friends don't really understand me. Sometimes I feel like I'm way over their heads.

8. I don't like it when somebody gives me the brush off for doing better than they do.

9. I have trouble coping with the way peers act. Sometimes they seem so dumb.

10. It's hard to ignore peer pressure without your friends thinking you're ignoring them.

You probably share all of these concerns and can add a few more of your own. And in the life of a teenager, they're a big deal. But let's tackle them one at a time. First, the teasing.

Teasing
The #1 Bummer

"Egghead." "The brain." "Junior Genius." "Weird." "Smarty." "Bookworm." These are just a few of the nicknames used on GTs and nobody appreciates them. Once armed with a label, teenagers often use it unmercilously. But don't think GTs are the only ones. No teenager escapes some form of teasing for being "different" — if your hair's red, or you're tall, short, fat, thin, have big boobs or a hairy chest or chew your food funny, or if your mother wears army boots, you can be sure you'll hear about it. You name it, somebody's got a label for it.

Why Teasing Is A Bummer

Make fun of adults, and if they're reasonably well adjusted, they'll likely shrug it off for what it's worth: an opinion (right or wrong), coming from somebody (they either respect or do not) about a subject or situation (which may or may not be important). Adults have had the experience needed to be able to evaluate situations for what they're worth. At teenage, it's likely you have not.

Everybody needs to feel they belong. You want to be OK, a part of the crowd, admired and accepted. You don't necessarily want to be *different*. And teasing sets you apart — frequently in a negative way.

This is where being a GT can zap you again. You get teased about being a brain. And when you reach your limit of teasing, you may begin to question whether being gifted is OK or not. You may even begin to wish that you weren't GT.

"When you're labeled gifted, if you do anything outside what people expect a gifted person to be, like go to a party and stay out late or get a C on a test, they think you're really weird. But if a jock stays out late or gets a C, nobody cares because it's OK for them to be different."

Holly, 15

Like Holly, if you don't feel like you belong anywhere, you're not going to be in a good position to use and develop your talents and abilities, to enjoy life to the fullest. It's likely you'll feel discouraged. And in that regard, GTs are not alone:

"I get tired of being called a brain all the time."

Amy, 13

"I'm not a social outcast or anything, but sometimes I feel people my age just don't understand me because I'm gifted. They tease me a lot. I wish my friends would accept giftedness as being a good thing."

Alice, 15

"I don't just get teased because I'm into school, I get bullied."

Tom, 13

"Some people call me a freak because I'm gifted. It's scary."

Diane, 17

"Even when labels are used in a teasing way, they are totally unindividualistic — which is the exact opposite of me."

Brett, 15

I am a snowman
All of the kids are playing with me
A few are jealous and try to make me feel bad
and they succeed. Then I do feel bad.
They press their advantage and finally, it
Becomes so hot with rumors about me
That I melt

Radhika, 11

All the lonely people,
where do they all belong?

John Lennon   1940-1980

How To Cope With Teasing

In order to effectively cope with teasing, you've got to realize that the problem comes from within *and* without. First, let's get a few things straight about being different from within.

It's perfectly OK to:

- Study a lot
- Love to read
- Learn about different things
- Get high grades
- Worry about world problems
- Be inquisitive
- Enjoy greater challenges
- Ask questions
- Use fun words

Obfuscate   sycophant   obstreperous

inure

strabismus

porte cochere   pleonastic   sodality

ululate

proficuous

exacerbate   lucubrate   modus   histrionic

frondiferous   banality

It's also OK to:
- Go to parties
- Get average grades
- Have dates
- Goof off
- Do dumb things
- See movies
- Sleep late
- Enjoy stuff that has nothing to do with school, learning, books, grades, etc.

Being different is just that. Being different. And being gifted is just one of the ways people can be different. Not *better* than. Not *worse* than. Just different.

I asked teenagers what advice they'd give their GT peers about the label, "gifted." This is what they said:

"I think gifted kids should be told that it's great to be gifted or talented. That you have many more opportunities open to you because of it."

"It isn't the label that counts. It's how you use it."

"You shouldn't compromise what you are just so that others will like you. You should make the most of yourself because life will be better for you in the long run."

"I made most of my friends in the advanced classes at school. Their goals and interests were compatible with mine and that's what made me feel so comfortable around them. Get into classes where you'll meet others who think like you."

"I get along with most everybody. I suppose there are people who don't like me and I'll never know why. But I try to be friendly to everyone and that makes life easier for me."

"It's not *bad* to be different. We're just different, that's all."

Once you come to believe that being GT is OK — that, in fact, it's fun to be different, then you can sort out the reasons why teasing may get you down.

I have endured a great deal of ridicule without much malice; and have received a great deal of kindness, not quite free from ridicule. I am used to it.

Abraham Lincoln

The whole issue of teasing is a problem with three parts. Ask yourself these questions the next time you're teased. If you understand how they work together, you can short-circuit the process and escape much of the emotional hurt that can result.

Effective Teasing Depends On:

1. **Who's doing the teasing**

2. **The reason why they're teasing**

3. **Whether you accept or reject it**

I. Who's Teasing

The principle villain in the teasing triangle is *who* is baiting the trap, not *what* was actually said.

Suppose somebody calls you a "junior genius." It makes a lot of difference whether *that* bit of teasing comes from: (1) your mom or dad; (2) somebody you hardly know; (3) a close friend; (4) a teacher; (5) your grandmother; (6) someone you don't respect.

And who said it has a great deal to do with whether you'll feel (a) hurt (b) angry (c) annoyed (d) amused (e) elated (f) like punching somebody's lights out (g) proud or whatever.

II. Why Friends Tease

The next step is to consider why your friends tease. Again, it should make a difference whether you're the brunt of some good-natured chiding or whether somebody really wants to put you down.

Five * Reasons Why Kids Tease GTs

1. Kids may be jealous of you. They, in fact, wish they could do as well.
2. Your friends may not know a better way of telling you they're proud of you and happy to be your friend. Teasing may be their way (peculiar as it seems) of saying "I think you're neat."
3. Some people regard being complimentary as "goody-goody." When you're a teenager, being goody-goody isn't cool so compliments are rare and teasing is the modus operandi.
4. Your peers may unconsciously feel inferior around you because they don't have enough good things going on in their own lives. Teasing is a way of putting you down so they feel better about themselves.
5. They don't like you.

*There may be more than five reasons. Feel free to add some of your own.

Obviously, you may not know exactly why a person is teasing you but you can appreciate the importance of the question. It makes a lot of difference whether someone teases you (1) because she's jealous; (2) because he doesn't like you; (3) because she doesn't know any better way to say, "I like you;" (4) because he or she is just plain dumb.

III. Accept or reject

At any rate, it is the combination of these elements which will determine how you're going to feel. If you accept the teasing without scrutiny, you may come away feeling like an outcast. Worse yet, you begin to wish you were anything but GT.

HOW GTS HANDLE TEASING

Remarkably few of the more than 300 gifted teenagers interviewed for this book had a specific strategy for handling teasing:

"When kids say, 'Oh, you're such a brain,' I just try to ignore it."

Brian, 14

●

"I just love to read and I read books faster than most people do. That bothers my friends and I'm not sure why. I try to ignore their remarks but when that doesn't work, I feel like hitting them."

Derek, 14

●

Thirteen-year-old Lynn, tells her detractors that "just because I get A's doesn't mean I'm smart."

●

"I was voted class brain so I'm constantly teased about being smart. But it's done in a fun way. I usually deny it when people say, 'Oh you're so smart.' I don't know what else to say. I don't want people to think I'm conceited."

Barb, 16

When being teased, always consider the source. Is the person who's teasing important to you? Do you respect them? If you don't, then your best shot is probably to ignore the comment and go on about your business. Try not to waste your time worrying.

If it's someone you really care about, evaluate why the person made the comment. And you may wish to clarify that situation by *asking* the person what they meant. After all, none of us is perfect. Could it be that you *really are* bragging too much about what a great student you are? On the other hand, it's possible the friend didn't mean anything by the comment at all. If not, he or she needs the opportunity to tell you so. Whatever the case, you may feel bad needlessly for not getting the whole picture.

Starting now, the next time you're the brunt of the teasing crew, think about *who's* doing it, *why* they're doing it, and *whether* it makes any difference to you or not.

Put some new sentences in your head using your questioning attitude. For example, let's assume somebody starts getting on your case because you got a C on a test instead of an A.

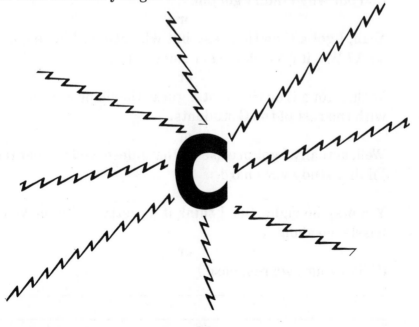

Rather than thinking:

A.) I got a C on the test
and
B.) my friend is making fun of me for not getting an A
therefore:
C.) I must be dumb, (or weird or inadequate)

Try thinking this:

A.) I got a C on a test
and
B.) my friend is making fun of me for not getting an A
therefore:
C.) You're right. I didn't do as well on this test as I might have. But I can afford to blow a test once in a while. After all, none of us is perfect.

or

Well, maybe you don't think I'm smart, but then again, your opinion isn't important to me.

or

Yes, I guess I did bomb that test. So what?

or

Actually, I deserved an A on that test. And I'm going to find out why I didn't get one.

or

Yeah, I got a C on that test, but why *should* I have gotten an A? Was it preordained or something?

or

Yeah, I got a C on that test. I guess they'll be arresting me with the rest of the C students.

or

Well, actually I got precisely what I deserved on that test. I didn't study very hard.

or

You may be right. But I think it's pretty tacky for you to hassle me about it.

or

(Fill in your own response.)

_____

_____

94

The point I'm trying to make here is that if you **automatically accept** the teasing that comes your way, you're not in control of your feelings — someone else is. You may or may not choose to believe what people say, but before you decide, question, challenge, work things through and *keep your own counsel.*

Fate chooses our relatives.
We choose our friends.
— Jacques Delille

"Friends" You Can Do Without

Even though we try to pick our friends carefully, everybody comes with good traits and bad ones. And sometimes the bad ones include cheating.

Gifted kids like you usually get involved because cheaters assume you know all the answers.

"My real friends don't ask me for help, but other kids do," confided 15-year-old Tracy. Her defense was to ignore the request.

And so it was for enough GTs to make it worth mentioning. Many get pestered for "extra help" on homework assignments.

"Kids don't ask me for help on tests so much as on assignments when they're too lazy to do it for themselves," said Jon, 14. Both GTs agreed that cheating on tests and helping on homework assignments were not frequent requests, but they did occur more often than they'd like. And when it happens to you, it's perfectly natural to feel uncomfortable.

What To Do When Friends Ask For Help

Examine your motivations for being a homework assistant. Many GTs feel good about being able to help others. They get a certain amount of pride when students (particularly popular ones), ask them questions. And if that's OK with you, go ahead and help.

But that's not the way it is all the time.

Sometimes "helping" becomes a hassle. And you'll ask yourself, "Should I or shouldn't I?"

Rather than giving you a long list of don'ts or shoulds, you might want to simply examine the consequences of helping others with their homework.

1. Helping can get out of hand. When it does, you may not have time to get your own work done. In which case, what do you do? You might politely turn down the request and level with the person: "I'd love to help you with your work but this week I just don't have time. Try me again, though."

2. Some people can take advantage of your help. You're the best judge of that. If it appears you're doing more work than they are, something's amiss.

3. Helping others can get you in trouble if classroom rules are violated in the process.

A friend who would ask you to do something dishonest is no friend at all.

"Help" on Tests

It's hardly worth talking about. You know what's right. You know who stands to lose if you get caught. Make up your own mind.

And if you decide not to cheat — just ignore the request. You don't need to explain why. The person whispering across the row or over your shoulders will know why.

> "Plant a new crop of friends each year."
> **John Brantner**

❀❀❀❀❀❀❀

Friends Who Think As You Do

Fully 80 percent of the GTs I interviewed said they feel more strongly about world problems than their peers. Things like the possibility of nuclear war, world hunger, pollution, international relations and the economy.

It's important to find some friends who think as you do because quite simply, it's a lonely sort of existence if you only have yourself to talk to.

For example, one girl told me that some of the people she knows "care more about their hair than the fact that we could all die from a nuclear war in the next few years. They just aren't concerned about anything outside their own little world," she complained.

Another student confessed that sometimes he wished he was not so intelligent because then maybe he wouldn't worry about things so much.

It's easy to start thinking there's something wrong with you if there isn't someone around who can relate on the same level.

Birds
Of A Feather

GTs need to be with others of similar interest and ability for at least part of the day.

One way to accomplish that is to be sure you're in at least one class for GT kids.

GTs in such classes unanimously agree that their gifted class is the one place they can really be themselves. They don't have to worry about using certain words for fear people will accuse them of showing off. They don't have to concern themselves with whether or not people understand what they were saying because it sounds "too sophisticated or philosophical." You can brainstorm without being judged a weirdo. Some GTs went so far as to say that their gifted class was *the* most important time of the week. They felt accepted.

But what do you do if your school doesn't have a gifted and talented education program? How do you find people who are "like" you?

Getting Close To
Big Kids

Many GTs solve that problem by finding accepting and similar-thinking adult friends.

Kids don't automatically value peers more than adults. But sometimes, young people feel alienated from adults simply because they don't have the opportunity to really get to know them. When they do, the experiences are most often good.

Some GTs found it easier to develop special relationships with parents, teachers, neighbors — any adult whose interests were in keeping with theirs.

Adults didn't accuse them of "showing off" their intellectual equipment; they didn't chide them because they were "different." Adult friends can be wiser, more objective, less judgmental than peers.

"I have a lot of trouble relating to kids my age. It's as though we're on a totally different wavelength."

Billy, 14, went on to admit, "I prefer adult company over kid company because I can contribute to their conversations without being thought of as strange for knowing what's going on."

Either way, whether you're hooking up with kids your own age or adults, you have to take the initiative.

TIPS ON MAKING NEW FRIENDS

You may feel you have enough friends right now. If so, that's great. But it you don't, and you want to make new friends, don't wait for somebody else to do it for you. And although this may sound preachy, the first step in making new friends is simply to *be* a friend.

> We secure our friends
> not by accepting favors,
> but by doing them.
>
> **Thucydides 460-400 B.C.**

To Wit:

1. Get involved. Join clubs of interest to you. Take special classes inside or outside of school.

2. Smile and say "hi" to people. (It sounds corny, I know, but you'll be amazed at the response you'll get when you extend a friendly greeting.)

3. Risk telling people about yourself. That doesn't mean bragging. But when it feels right, let your interests be known. For example, if you love reading science fiction, and you would like to know others who love sci fi, spread the word around.

4. Learn to be more accepting of others and remember that even though someone doesn't always agree with you, they can still be interesting and fun to be with.

5. Remember that practice makes perfect. Sometimes things you try won't work. People aren't born with social skills, they have to be developed. Each time you risk getting to know someone, you'll learn a little about how to get the best results. The things that are important to people in their friendships aren't any big secret. But it does take two to tango. In other words, and I've said it before, you have to be a friend to have a friend.

Barb, 16, says this about her relationships with friends, "My friends and I support each other and when someone is down, we try to bring them up by saying life's too short not to spend it being happy." Brian, 14, adds that it's "important to spend a lot of time with friends. They need to know you're there."

6. Friends are everywhere and can be made anywhere. School is only one of those places. Many states have organizations that advocate for the gifted and talented. Some of these groups have conferences for GTs where you can meet people who share your thinking and your interests. (See the resource section for more information.)

I get by with a little help from my friends
— **Paul McCartney**

"It's a great advantage to be gifted. Sometimes you feel like you're really alone, but you're not. It's great to be your own person and you shouldn't try to be like everyone else, just so people will like you. It's very important not to let your talents slip through your fingers by trying to fit in with everybody. Rather, you should find friends who complement your abilities.
Rene, 15

HOME
SWEET HOME

Being gifted can not only change your relationships with classmates and friends, it can often play havoc with life at home (surprise, surprise?)

Mother, father, sisters, brothers, they all get into your act. Sometimes it's about things that all families hassle over: chores, homework, curfews, eating habits, clothes, hair styles, etc. But sometimes it's about being gifted.

> "Everyone expects so much of you
> when you're gifted."
>
> Tony, 14

The "everybody" that Tony was talking about was his parents. And by far and away the biggest complaint about parents was the tremendous pressure they exert over GTs to not just do *well*, but to be *perfect*.

This quest for perfection can manifest itself in many ways.
- They expect you to study every night
- Parents try to control the kinds of courses you take
- They expect you to get straight A's
- They expect you to behave perfectly

"My biggest hassle in life right now is that I *always* have to be totally responsible. To please my parents, I have to stay home and work instead of being with friends. I don't see why they can't understand that I can be responsible and spend some time with my friends too."

Jan, 15

"Trying to do everything that's expected of you, and doing it perfectly because you're gifted, is a big problem for me. It's like I'm not a good person if I flub up."

Chuck, 14

"My parents expect too much of me. They constantly tell me to do homework when I'm already getting straight A's. It doesn't make sense to me."

Mike, 16

"My parents stress law, business or medicine and look upon the arts as a waste of time. I have a terrible time putting together what I want to do and what my parents want me to do."

Esther, 17

You've probably felt the brunt of this sort of pressure too. Parents who just can't get it into their heads that you're not perfect, that in many ways, you're just a normal kid. But most importantly, you want to live *your* life, not theirs.

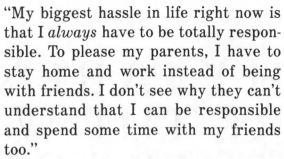

WHY PARENTS ARE THE WAY THEY ARE

The next time your parent(s) start doing a perfection number on you, we've got several suggestions for how to handle it. First, get a grip on where your parents might be coming from. If you can understand their motivation, (however misguided), you'll be in a better position to negotiate change in your favor. Please notice we didn't say it was *right* for them to feel this way. We just said they do it. Some parents believe that if they have high expectations of you, they'll stand a better chance of seeing you live up to those expectations. (Meaning they've done a great job). Moreover, this technique often works so they keep doing it.

1. First of all, parents often see themselves reflected in their kids. That means if you get A's, big awards and commendations and the like, *they* (vicariously) get A's, big awards and commendations. If you're well-behaved, it must mean that your parents are good, too.

   On the other hand, if you don't give a rip about getting A's, awards and commendations, your parents may take it personally. They may feel that they've failed in some way. That they're lousy parents.

2. Sometimes, parents make great demands on you in order to fulfill their *personal* hopes and dreams. For example, a parent who always wanted to go to college and never made it, may push you to go to college — whether you want to or not. Or a parent may think that a particular occupation (usually, their own) is so wonderful they push you to follow the same path.

3. Maybe one or both of your parents is GT. A common characteristic of GTs at any age is the imposition of high standards on themselves. This self-imposed perfectionism may be carried down to you. Does this sound familiar? "If *I* can do it, *you* can do it."

4. Another reason parents may have unreasonably high expectations of you is that they sometimes forget that teenagers are just that — teenagers.

You may unwittingly contribute to the expectation that you should behave as an adult, not as a teenager. Take this mini-quiz and see what I mean:

? Do you sometimes prefer adult company over peers?

? Do you have friends who are several years older than you?

? Do you have conversations with your parents and other adults about world issues like the ones we mentioned earlier?

? Are you fairly responsible for yourself?

When you spend time with adults, talk like an adult, and sometimes think like an adult, parents (naturally) start perceiving you as an adult. But in reality, you're only partly adult.

When you behave as an adult, that's cool. When you don't — you'll hear about it:

"With your intelligence, I would have expected you to:
act more maturely, or
be more responsible, or
stop this silliness, or
act your age."

TURNOFF

Now that you know a few of the reasons *why* parents get on your case about being perfect, what can you do about it?

First, a word about what doesn't work. Here are seven statements guaranteed to turn your parents off. Cold.

1. You *always* want me to be perfect. (Especially in a whiny voice.)
2. But that's not fair.
3. But none of the other guys . . .
4. Can't I do it next week (next month, next year, next . . .)?
5. You're just trying to get me to be like you.
6. You *NEVER* understand anything.
7. Just because you grew up in the Stone Age . . .

So much for what *doesn't* work. Now a few words about what *does*.

First, a few easy rules about coping with your parents high expectations.

 "What we've got here is a failure to communicate."

from Cool Hand Luke

COPING WITH GREAT EXPECTIONS

1. The most helpful thing in getting parents to have realistic expectations of you, according to gifted teenagers who have succeeded in doing it, is talk. Talk, talk and more talk. Not argue. Talk. No door slamming. Talk. Try to see their point of view. Explain how you feel about their expectations. Share the good stuff and the bad stuff. (We've got a complete plan about how to do that later in this section.)

2. As a GT, you run the risk of doing a number on yourself without help from anyone else — so take it easy.

   "If you have success most of the time, and then you fail at something, you may get very frustrated. This is one of the greatest problems facing gifted kids."

   Julie, 12

3. Trust yourself and don't let what other people think control you. After all, you have to live with your decisions. Obviously, that doesn't mean you should ignore your parents' counsel. They do have more experience in life. And we all have to abide by some rules. But whenever possible, try to make your own decisions and be ready to accept responsibility for the consequences.

4. You do not have to "do your best" all of the time — contrary to popular opinion. Sometimes it isn't even practical to do so. When parents encourage you to be best, talk it over with them. Evaluate why you may or may not want to strive for perfection. Doing a good job may more often than not be important, but it needn't be your *raison d'être*.

5. Encourage your parent(s) to learn more about what being GT means. Get information for them if you have to and make sure that you've read it too so you can discuss it with them. If they aren't interested in knowing more, at least you'll have a greater awareness and acceptance of yourself by learning as much as you can.

6. If there's absolutely no way you can get through to your parents, don't be afraid to get support from another adult. Not everyone is blessed with cooperative, supportive parents. We wish it were that way but in fact, some of us have to look elsewhere for role models. And that's OK. These people could be other relatives, teachers, school counselors, neighbors, camp counselors or some other member of the community.

How To Get More Freedom

Frequently, GTs mature faster than their parents are willing to admit. The result? A painful gap between what GTs *want* to do and what their parents will *allow* them to do.

Among these freedoms are:

How late you can stay up

Places you can go

Choosing your friends

The classes you take

The after-school activities you pursue

The way you spend your money

What to do with your life

Obviously, there are a lot more you could add, but suffice to say, you don't want to wait until you're 18 before you're allowed to take advantage of life's opportunities. You want it all right now.

What do parents say about all that?

The parents I've talked to expressed difficulty in knowing how much freedom they can allow without being too permissive (or too restrictive).

Without guidelines, all hell breaks loose. Too many guidelines feels like a prison sentence. Too few and nobody gets what they want.

The answer lies somewhere in between and it's complicated by the fact that you're at that in-between stage in your life when freedoms often come begrudgingly.

If you want to gain greater freedom, if you want to "do your own thing," a level of trust and confidence has to be built. Your parents need to know that you can handle the freedom you request. They can gauge your ability to handle more freedom by evaluating how well you assume the responsibilities you have right now. For example, do you:

Usually get your homework done _____?
Keep your room clean _____?
Handle your money wisely _____?
Take proper care of your library card _____?
Buy your own clothes _____?
Tell the truth _____?

If you're keeping up your end of the bargain, you're in a stronger position to negotiate for more freedom.

Set up a meeting with your parents to discuss your concern. Express a desire to take on more responsibility. Lay out your plan and try to come to a concensus about what it is that you want. Here are some tips for negotiating with parents:

1. **Pick a time** that is agreeable to everyone. Make an appointment if necessary to assure the meeting will happen. Be sure to show up on time.

2. **Choose a comfortable place** for your meeting. Obviously, if the TV is blaring, the phone ringing and your little brother is being a nuisance, it's going to be tough to accomplish anything. How about meeting in a park, going out for a walk, or using a conference room at the public library?

3. **Make an agenda** for your meeting. Write down some points you wish to make. Many times, in discussions like these, we tend to forget some of the things we wanted to say. An agenda will jog your memory.
4. **Keep it upbeat.** This is not a gripe session. For a meeting to be productive, you've got to exchange viewpoints, *negotiate*, compromise and plan for action. What is each person willing to do?
5. **Try, try again.** It's only natural that if you're just now trying to open the lines of communication, you might get a few wires crossed during your debut as a negotiator. But don't let this discourage you.

If you don't succeed at first . . .

Don't be afraid to enjoy the stress of a full life
nor be too naive to think you can do so without some
intelligent thinking and planning. Man should not
try to avoid stress any more than he would shun food
or love or exercise.

Hans Selye

Stress caused by giftedness
and what to do about it

In trying to be your own person and do your own thing, there will be conflicts with the establishment. We've talked about many situations that present challenges to GTs: the school system, teachers, parents, classmates or others.

When these conflicts occur, it's likely that you will suffer from stress or anxiety. It's the body's way of telling you that you don't feel quite right about the way things are going. Or perhaps you feel elated about a particular event. Believe it or not, excitement is a form of stress.

It's important to note that all stress isn't bad. In fact, a certain amount of stress enables us to improve our performance, increase productivity and ultimately get more out of life.

But if the stress you're experiencing goes beyond what could be categorized as mild, or if mild stress is *prolonged,* your physical and mental health will be jeopardized.

The consequences of prolonged or intense stress are varied. But generally speaking, people without appropriate outlets for coping with undue anxiety or strain exhibit one or more of the following behaviors:

nervousness
excessive daydreaming
apathy
laziness
withdrawal

chemical abuse
truancy
vandalism
hostility
thoughts of suicide

To determine if you are suffering from stress, use this checklist. Check the blanks to show when, if ever, you experience the following symptoms of stress:

Physical stress	Often	Sometimes	Never
Headaches			
Stomachaches			
Fatigue			
Backaches			
Appetite changes			
Other			
Class hassles			
A drop in grades			
Loss of concentration			
Loss of memory abilities			
Withdrawal from your usual activities			
Dealing with others:	Often	Sometimes	Never
Are you becoming a loner?			
Do you feel compelled to join in everything and be everywhere?			
Mood Swings			
Happy to depressed			
Are you often irritable?			
Bored with *everything?*			
Do you feel worthless?			
Are you argumentative?			
Other symptoms:			
Trouble getting to sleep			
Sleeping too much			
Worry a lot			
Nightmares			
Thoughts of suicide			
Stealing			

Only you can decide whether or not stress is becoming bad news in your life. But if you've checked "often" in any instance, we recommend that you move on to the next step, and perhaps even seek professional help in order to help yourself feel better.

If you've frequently checked "sometimes" you may also have cause for concern.

The bottom line is, do you feel OK? if you do — no sweat. If you don't, read on.

Now let's take a look at what *causes* stress. In their own words, GTs feel stressed when they:

- Suffer an excessive fear of failure.
- Don't fit in with other kids.
- Have too many options when it comes to choosing a career.
- Burn out from trying to do too much.
- Get impatient with routine, dull classes.
- Have to live up to the expectations of self or others.
- Have difficulty making friends who accept them.
- Compete with siblings or classmates.
- Have few challenges in school.
- Are teased about being gifted and talented.
- Have to do their best day in and day out.

To begin reducing stress, it's important for you to list the specific things which create anxiety or pressure in *your* life. Your list may include some of the things felt by other GTs. Take time to think about your most stress-producing situations.

I feel anxious when:

1. _____
2. _____
3. _____
4. _____
5. _____

Now that you've got a handle on what the symptoms of stress look like and what causes anxiety, let's get on with the business of keeping your cool.

"It has been proved by my own experience that every problem carries within itself its own solution, a solution to be reached only by the intense inner concentration of a severe devotion to truth."
Frank Lloyd Wright

The majority of GTs left me with the impression that someone else was responsible for their stressful situations, and that they were powerless to make changes. And that seemed to be the feeling whether the problem was related to school, a certain teacher, parents, future career choices or their lack of friends.

But that notion is a cop out. *We* are responsible for the way things go in our lives. *We* own our feelings and must accept that no one can help us cope with stress unless we take the initiative to do what needs to be done. (You've already got a head start by reading this chapter!)

Reducing GT Stress

There are three (at least) ways to reduce stress: (1) You can eliminate the problem causing the stress; (2) You can change your attitude toward the problem; (3) You can reduce the anxiety you're feeling by engaging in stress-reducing activity.

Here's an example. Suppose being teased causes stress for you. Here are three possible solutions. You can: Convince the person to stop teasing you. Change your attitude so that teasing doesn't bother you or accept the teasing and then "work off" the stress it creates by taking a run or talking about the problem in a GT class.

Now Let's See How
That Works In Real Life

Todd B. told me that taking tests really got him uptight. He learned to relax by setting up a method for preparing for tests. He realized that his anxiety occurred when he felt unprepared for exams. In order to alleviate as much of the stress as possible, he simply made sure that he knew his stuff. He, in effect, eliminated the problem. Todd obviously had several alternatives. He could, for example, have decided that tests just weren't important to him but chose instead to opt for solving the problem.

Through trial and error you'll find out what works in your life. Just remember: If it works, it's (probably) right.

There are a number of other ways Todd might have reduced his stress.

For example, a few GTs mentioned that doing something physical like running or walking seemed to help. Some read books to escape from the problem, even if temporarily. Others found writing in a journal to be comforting. It enabled them to reflect on their feelings and to think about what was going on.

Here are some other stress-reducing activities you might try:

- Go to a movie
- Take a nap
- Talk to somebody you don't know
- Slug something (not somebody)
- Go for a ride
- Go to church
- Wander through a bookstore
- Call a relative
- Work on a hobby
- Do something nice for somebody
  (and don't get found out!)

Helpful Hints

- Try to remember past situations where you've been successful in coping with an unnerving event. You may be able to reuse those same strategies in a new situation and be successful again.
- Learn how to handle pressures without alienating others. (Obviously, one way to eliminate stress caused by a demanding teacher would be to eliminate him or her. That is, however, a bit extreme.) You don't necessarily need to conform, but making others feel inferior or bad won't help anyone, least of all you. Speak on behalf of others as well as yourself.
- Get a mentor, or other support person to serve as a sounding board. This person should be someone you can count on for honesty and trustworthiness.
- If you don't know how to relax, learn how. Good physical and mental health demands that we spend at least some time daily reflecting and slowing down. Consider daydreaming, meditation, prayer, listening to music (hard rock probably isn't the best choice but if it works for you . . .), going for leisurely walks, craft work, anything that fits into the category of, as one boy put it, "something that doesn't require my brain to work too hard."
- Keep trying. Coping with stress is a learned skill and doesn't happen overnight. Your stress-handling techniques will be modified as you experience new things, but having specific techniques to use should become part of your routine.
- When in doubt, look on the bright side of things. A smile never hurts.

Finally, remember that you don't have to go it alone. There's always somebody around who's willing to listen, there's always a place to go for help. Here are just a few suggestions:
- A supportive adult
- A friendly neighbor
- A teen clinic
- A crisis intervention center
- Emergency hotlines
- The public library
- Stress management class
- Your favorite friend
- A counselor

If I have to,
I can do anything,
I am strong,
I am invincible,
I am woman.
— **Helen Reddy**

Got A Problem?

"You're Either Part of the Solution or Part of the Problem."
— Eldridge Cleaver

Creative Problem Solving, while the result of a number of learning specialists, was the brainchild of Dr. Alex Osborn and Dr. Sidney Parnes.

Osborn, an advertising executive, and Parnes, a professor of creative studies, developed a way for people to maximize their creative abilities and solve problems.

The five-step CPS technique goes like this:

1. Determine the facts
2. Analyze the problem
3. Brainstorm potential solutions
4. Evaluate potential solutions
5. Select and carry out a solution

Sounds easy, doesn't it? Well, maybe. Many GTs find CPS to be a rather complicated, Mickey Mouse process for something they do quite simply and naturally by themselves. Take a close look at the steps. See if you're one of these GTs. Again, if it works for you, great! If not, try something else.

123

Step 1 — Determine the facts

By determining what facts are involved with your problem, you can see the whole picture. Rarely is a problem just one problem. Things are usually more complicated than that.

To clarify the problem, list what it is you want to change or accomplish as completely as possible. Be specific. To do that, ask yourself the five W's. (Who? What? When? Where? And How?) For example:

Who's always bugging you about grades? Is it Mom, Dad, a teacher?

When does it happen? All the time? Only at report card time? How do they bug you?

You should be able to outline the six facets of the problem before you move to Step Two.

Step 2 — Analyze the problem

Here's where you begin to take a closer look at the problem. Ask Why?

My dad expects me to get all A's because _____
_____ .

Then, choose the statement that best describes the problem.

Step 3 — Brainstorm potential solutions

In case you're unfamiliar with the rules for brainstorming, we've listed them for you. You may want to tear this part of the book out to keep yourself on target whenever you brainstorm.

"Allow your imagination to soar before engineering down to earth."
Alex Osborn

Brainstorming

List as many solutions to the problem as possible. While brainstorming:
* *Defer judgment of ideas, criticism is taboo.
* *List as many ideas as possible. Quantity breeds quality.
* *Be zany, far-out, free — every idea is accepted.
* *Combine or improve upon ideas, piggyback, substitute things, magnify, minify, eliminate, reverse.

CAUTION: Don't give up when there's a lull in production — this is usually a break between obvious and new ideas.

Step 4 — Evaluate potential solutions

Now take a look at all of the possible solutions you have. Evaluate each idea according to your needs and values. Weigh each idea against the factors which will make the solution possible or impossible. Things to consider might be:

Time involved
Cost
How many people it takes to carry it out
Legal or illegal?
Moral?
How much effort is needed?

Now, choose the solution which *best* solves the problem.

Step 5 — Select and carry out a solution

This is when your work pays off. You should now have a solution to your problem. All that's left is to put it to good use.

Finally, here are some tips for Creative Problem Solving:

1. If a terrific solution comes to mind before you get to the end of the CPS exercise, by all means go with it. There's no need to go through all of these steps unless you have to.

2. While doing CPS, you may get stuck or come up against new problems. When that happens, you may have to start over again to get a fresh perspective.

3. CPS can be done by one person or a group. If you're working in a group, ideas "belong" to the group, not individuals. That way, the group judges ideas, *not* people.

4. Brainstorming isn't just for GTs. Most everyone can learn to do it. But for you to get from potential to achievement, it's a skill you can't do without.

5. Don't expect to be skilled at CPS immediately. Practice will enable you to improve your technique.

6. Have fun!

Sticking Up For Your Rights

There's been a lot of talk in this book about making changes. And that's all well and good — unless you don't have the guts to *make* the changes. And that's what this section of the book is about: How to become assertive so you get what you want.

There have been lots of books written about assertiveness and if you've got a mind to know a whole lot about the subject we recommend you read *Your Perfect Right* (by Robert Alberti and Michael Emmons) or *The Assertive Woman* (by Stanlee Phelps and Nancy Austin).

But if you want just a short course on the subject, we can help.

Knowing Your Rights

Obviously, the beginning point in any plan designed to help you assert your rights is to determine what rights you have — as a human being, and as a GT teenager.

Certainly, for example, we are guaranteed by law certain inalienable rights:

The right to act as we want, as long as we don't injure ourselves or others; the right to own and express our views and opinions, the right to say no, the right to be respected, the right to have needs as important as other peoples', and so on.

We also have rights as GTs — and these are the ones this book is concerned with.

Remember the Eight Great Gripes? Well, we have a right to live WITHOUT the Eight Great Gripes.

Eight Great Rights

I. You have a right to attend classes which are as interesting as they are challenging.

II. You have a right to do your best work when you want to and less than perfect work when you don't.

III. You have a right to have friends who really understand you.

IV. You have a right to pursue relevant schoolwork at your own speed.

V. You have a right to be treated with respect by friends, teachers and parents.

VI. You have a right to freedom of choice regarding your life's ambitions.

VII. You have a right to be different.

VIII. You have a right to be concerned with life on Earth and have opportunities for making it better.

As you know from reading this book, many times GTs are not given their rights. And unless somebody gives them to you, you're going to have to *demand them*. And that's easier said than done.

Why? Because you may not know how to do it; or you may feel intimidated by people.

GTs Fail To Be Assertive Because:

- They don't understand or are uncertain about their rights.
- They're not sure what they want.
- They're afraid that when others disagree, they'll appear stupid or unreasonable.
- They've been shot down before and are afraid to take the risk again.

What Assertiveness Isn't:

Many people have funny ideas about what being assertive is all about. Oftentimes, they get it confused with a lot of things that it isn't. For example, assertiveness is not:

Aggressiveness That means winning at *all* costs; sticking up for your rights — even if you trample over the rights of others to get them.

Passivity Simply put, this is the opposite of what you want to do. You do not want to dilly-dally waiting for *others* to act.

Hostility Being loud, rude or obnoxious to make your point. Simple, firm, non-threatening action will serve you far better.

OK, so what *is* assertive behavior?

Assertiveness means standing up for your personal rights in direct, honest and sincere ways while respecting the rights and opinions of others.

Learning to be assertive doesn't happen overnight. It takes time, patience and practice, practice, practice.

If you feel you haven't been very assertive in your dealings with friends, family or teachers, here are a few do's and don'ts to get you started:

DO: 1) Think about a situation you'd like to change. Start with a small, simple one to maximize your chances of success.
2) Decide who is alienating your right. Consider his or her position so you can be fully prepared.
3) Review what you want to say and request of this person. Go over it in your mind and visualize yourself actually doing it.
4) Observe others who are assertive. Analyze their approach. What are their keys to success?
5) Anticipate what might happen and be ready with backup statements.
6) Choose the best time to approach the person and give it a try.
7) If you're successful, think about the steps you took so you can have repeat performances. If things didn't go as planned and you didn't get what you wanted, figure out what went wrong to avoid making the same mistake next time.

DON'T: 1) Procrastinate
2) Place blame — it won't help
3) Get off track, keep your focus
4) Make threats (it only backs people into a corner)
5) Be unwilling to compromise
6) Stop trying

None of us are ever assertive 100 percent of the time. Sometimes there's no need to be. But when your needs and rights aren't being met, it's nice to know that you can stand up, be heard, and get what you want.

How does it feel, to be on your own
With no direction home
Like a complete unknown
Like a rolling stone?

Bob Dylan, *Like A Rolling Stone*

Setting Goals

A common characteristic of successful gifted adults is that they set goals for themselves. They've learned to be responsible for making things happen and don't wait for others to tell them what to do or to do things for them.

Charles Garfield, a University of California performance psychologist, agreed. He identified goal setting and five other characteristics common to the 1200 high achievers he researched. This is what he found:

- They are able to transcend previous accomplishments.
- They avoid the comfort zones, a no-mans land where they feel at home.
- They do it for the art, and are guided by internal goals.
- They solve problems instead of place blame.
- They take risks confidently, but only after laying out the worst consequences beforehand.
- They rehearse coming events mentally, using imagery.

Unlike Garfield's findings, only a small percentage of the GTs I've worked with have been committed goal setters. Most GTs, unfortunately, have come to believe that responsibility means doing what you're told (or what is expected of you) — no more and no less. As a result, many have not learned to take charge of their lives.

True responsibility means exerting control over your life by getting in touch with what *you* want to accomplish, making plans to get there and following through with those plans.

While concern for others is implicit, and we should consider how what we do affects others, living someone else's goals and dreams is hardly a satisfying, healthy way to live.

Why set goals? What's in it for you?

Initially, setting goals may seem like a lot of work or you may wonder, "how can I set goals when I don't know what I want to do?" But people who plan are convinced that this is the way to get more out of life. Here are some of the rewards you can expect to appreciate:

1. Setting goals and following them through will give you independence. There may not be a person nearby who can teach you what you want to learn. With goal-setting, you don't have to wait for someone else to decide your life for you, you're in the driver's seat.
2. It's been demonstrated over and over that people who are self-directed more often reach their goals. They don't *wish* things would occur, they *make* them occur.
3. When you set goals and carry them through, you feel a greater sense of accomplishment than if another person tells you what to do.
4. By taking charge of your life, you'll learn how to manage time more effectively and as a result, you'll get more done.
5. People who make plans and do things aren't bored and they aren't boring.

Getting Started

The first thing you need when setting goals is uninterrupted time and a place free from interference. If that means going for a walk in the woods or isolating yourself in the library, then do it.

Bring along several sheets of paper or a notebook and begin to arrange your goals in terms of short-, medium-, and long-range plans.

For example, write down all the things you'd like to do during the next ten years. You might write down (1) a college education; (2) a trip to Europe; (3) get married; (4) have children; (5) get a good job, and so on. Try to be as thorough and specific as possible. Take as much time as you want.

When you've got the list completed, prioritize your long-range goals and select the most important three or four. And write them on the bottom of your page.

Next, do the same thing for your intermediate goals, those for around 3-5 years. Write down as many as you can, prioritize and select only the top three or four.

Lastly, do the same things for your immediate goals: things you want to accomplish in the next year or so. Again, prioritize and select the top few.

Ideally your short-range goals should relate directly to accomplishing your medium-range goals. And your medium-range goals should help you achieve long-range goals. If they don't, something's wrong.

And that's where most goal-setting falls apart. Lots of kids (and adults) have a general idea of where they might like to be five, ten or fifty years from now. But they do not have the discipline to do the *daily* planning to accomplish all the "little things" that long-range goals are made of.

If you're having that sort of problem, I'd recommend you read a copy of *How To Get Control Of Your Time And Your Life* by Alan Lakein. It's an excellent guide to getting things done and I think you'll enjoy it. In the meantime, here are some suggestions to help you along the way!

> *. . . You've got to plant some seeds,*
> *and you'd better plant a lot of them,*
> *cause you can't tell which ones will*
> *sprout.*
> — **David Campbell**

- Be prepared to achieve *some* of your goals but not all of them. We live in an ever-changing, imperfect world so save yourself some unnecessary grief and accept that nothing is ever going to be permanent. We have the most control over the short-term goals and the least control over long-term goals. That's why you have to plant a lot of seeds. If one thing doesn't work out for you, you'll have plenty of other stuff going on to keep you going.
- Free yourself to change goals as interests, resources and other factors warrant. (Obviously, if one of your goals is to go to the library every Saturday and you later find out that it isn't open on weekends, something has to change.)
- Be honest with yourself. Learn to recognize the deceptive ways of thinking that will get in the way of being responsible for yourself. Common statements that trip people are:

I can't	versus	I don't want to try. I'm afraid.
I don't have the time	versus	I choose not to make time. It's not a priority for me.
Why me?	versus	Why not me?
This school is boring	versus	I'm bored. What can I do to remedy the situation?

- When in doubt, trust your intuition. Gut feelings can carry you through when things become difficult or unclear.

- Being self-directed doesn't mean you don't need others. It doesn't mean you have power over others either. Help others to feel good about themselves and what they're doing while you're enjoying life's amenities.

- Practice, practice, practice — until goal setting and following through become part of your lifestyle.

- Share goals with a friend. Have a support person.

- Be ready to hold fast to your convictions. Ask yourself if you're confident enough to go on with your plans even if someone doesn't approve or like your ideas. If not, better check your reasons for doing what you're doing. Maintaining your beliefs can sometimes be lonely in the face of peer or other pressures. But it doesn't need to be intolerable. As one girl advised,

"Don't give up your dreams because of what other kids say. Stick with your goals because you have to live with them."

And that's what this book has been all about: making plans and seeing your dreams come true.

No, it isn't easy. And no, there aren't any guarantees. But we hope you now have some of the knowledge you'll need to understand, accept, and celebrate your giftedness. We hope, that with the help of this book, you'll be able to carve a bigger, more delectable and challenging slice of life for yourself. Enjoy!

> "Cheshire-Puss," . . . said Alice, "would you tell me, please, which way I ought to go from here?"
> "That depends a good deal on where you want to get to," said the Cat.
> "I don't much care where — " said Alice.
> "Then it doesn't matter which way you go," said the Cat.
> " — so long as I get somewhere," Alice added as an explanation.
> "Oh, you're sure to do that," said the Cat. "if you only walk long enough."

> — Lewis Carroll,
> *Alice's Adventures in Wonderland*

APPENDIX

Everything You Ever Wanted To Know About Giftedness — And More

Within the confines of this book, we've just touched the surface of what being GT is all about. If you or your parents want to know more, there are a number of organizations that can provide you with all sorts of information: from special topics on underachievers and career counseling for GTs to alternative schools and parent education programs.

Each of these organizations has their own newsletter and offers other publications (books and pamphlets) as well. I've found them ready and willing to help.

Many states in the U.S. have directors of gifted education. To find out if your state has such a person, call or write NACG below and they can give you the complete lowdown.

The World Council for the Gifted and Talented, Inc.
HMS Rm. 414
University of South Florida
Tampa, FL 33620 • (813) 974-3638

NAGC, The National Association for Gifted Children
P.O. Box 66365
Washington, D.C. 20035

CEC, The Council for Exceptional Children
1920 Association Drive
Reston, VA 22091 • (703) 620-3660

The National State Leadership Training
Institute on the Gifted and Talented (N/S-LTI-G/T)
One Wilshire Bldg. — Suite 1007
Los Angeles, CA 90017-3311 • (213) 489-7470

Mind Expanding Magazines

If you're after some reading that will be insightful, futuristic, creative, extraordinary or all of the above — here are a few magazines sure to pique your interest:

- *Creative Kids* — Fun, clever, colorful, reflective. This magazine is jam-packed with stories, art, cartoons, poems, articles, games, interviews, photographs and more. It's produced *by* and *for* GTs and I think it's great. Really worth looking into. (Would the school library be willing to subscribe?)

- *The Futurist* — This magazine is published by the World Future Society. Can you guess what it's about? It offers forecasts, trends and ideas about all aspects of the future: life styles, values, technology, government, economics, the environment, etc. No doubt about it this is pretty heavy stuff but if you don't believe in crystal balls, this journal may be for you.

- *Games* — On the lighter side, *Games* is for those who really like to strrrretch their minds. If offers games, puzzles, logic problems, reader contests and reviews of new board and video games, at varying degrees of difficulty. Great for mental gymnastics of the best kind.

- *National Geographic World* — Who doesn't know about the fabulous and colorful National Geographic Magazine? This one, however, is produced for kids (8 years and over). It's filled with articles about nature and wildlife, exploration and science, sports and hobbies, pets and kids from all over the world. They also weave mazes, games and puzzles into each issue.

- *Saturday Review* — This is for those of you who truly appreciate the fine arts: books, theater, music, dance and film. Pretty cultural stuff done in a format of previews and reviews, articles and interviews. Any serious writer/arts person should be at least familiar with this magazine.

- *Natural History* — Definitely thought-provoking and informative. Written for everyone, (not just readers with super-sophisticated tastes,) it contains articles about conservation, the "natural" world, and the human environment. Heavily illustrated with photographs and drawings, it does a great job of presenting problems facing our world. *Natural History* also reviews books and has a regular column for astronomy enthusiasts and naturalists.
- *OMNI* — Thirty percent science fiction and seventy percent science according to the editors. If you seek greater understanding of science and have a passion for sci-fi, this may be the book for you. (I say book because it doesn't really seem like a magazine and the price is bookish too!) *OMNI* uses a broad spectrum of articles, essays, graphics and illustrations to inform its readers about earth, life, space, UFOs, the mind, etc. I have to admit, it does boggle my mind.

*Mailing addresses are listed in case you can't find these magazines at newsstands.

Creative Kids—GCT, Inc.
     Box 6448
     Mobile, AL 36660

The Futurist—World Future Society
     4916 St. Elmo Avenue
     Bethesda, MD 20814

Games—PSC Publications
     810-7th Avenue
     New York, NY 10019

National Geographic World— 17th & M Sts. NW
          Washington, D.C. 20036

Saturday Review Magazine—Penthouse International Ltd.
          1965 Broadway
          New York, NY 10023

Natural History—Central Park W. at 79th St.
     New York, NY 10024

OMNI—Penthouse International Ltd.
     1965 Broadway
     New York, NY 10023

Here are some books I recommend:

Changing Bodies, Changing Lives, Ruth Bell, Random House, 1987.

This book is for teenagers and offers frank information about human sexuality and body development. It doesn't judge but will help you to understand and trust your own feelings so that you'll have more control over your future. It's full of quotes from other teenagers who are changing and experiencing some of the same things you are. For the whole truth and nothing but the truth, read this book.

Perfectionism: What's Bad About Being Too Good, by Miriam Adderholdt-Elliott, Free Spirit Publishing Inc., 1987.

If you often feel that nothing you do is good enough then this book is for you. *Perfectionism* explores the problem of perfectionism and offers strategies to think about and try. The book is encouraging, realistic, and emphasizes the importance of who you are (vs. what you do).

Where The Sidewalk Ends: Poems & Drawings, Shel Silverstein, Harper and Row Publishers, 1974.

This book is pure pleasure. If you like poetry (and especially if you *don't* like poetry) you'll love this book. Silverstein's whacky artwork is terrific too. This book is great for laughs and for keeping life in perspective.

Turning People On: How to Be an Encouraging Person, Lewis E. Losoncy, Prentice-Hall, Inc., 1977.

This book is all about how to motivate other people, and more importantly, how to motivate yourself as well. It's practical and has step-by-step exercises throughout the book. It really left me feeling good about myself. What more could you ask for?

Attention Parents

More than just talk . . . Here's action!

If you want specific methods for developing and strengthening communication and cooperation between the members of your family, I highly recommend these two pamphlets. They're practical, short and *very* affordable. Each booklet contains recommendations for further reading, too.

Winning Teenagers Over in Home and School
By Francis X. Walton, Ph.D.

and

The Family Council
By Kleona B. Rigney, M.D. and Raymond J. Corsini, Ph.D.

Both are available from: The Alfred Adler Institute, 1841 Broadway
New York, NY 10023

CREDITS

Addresses for programs for the gifted and talented mentioned in the book are:

The Mentor Connection
Metro ECSU
3499 Lexington Ave. N.
St. Paul, MN 55126
(612) 490-0058

West Suburban Summer School
   Association for the Gifted and Talented
Intermediate District 287
1820 Xenium Lane
Plymouth, MN 55441
(612) 553-5667

The Autonomous Learning Publications and Specialists (ALPS)
P.O. Box 2264
Greeley, CO 80632
(303) 352-1414

Enrichment/Independent Study
Clearview Junior High School
Breakneck Rd.
Mullica Hill, NJ 08062
(609) 478-4400

Information on the Creative Problem Solving Process (CPS) was derived from *Applied Imagination*, Alex Osborn. Scribners, 1963 and *The Magic of Your Mind* by Sidney Parnes. The Creative Education Foundation, 1981.

Student quotes about Advance Placement reprinted with permission from *What College Students Say About Advanced Placement* by Patricia Lund Casserly. Copyright © 1968 by the College of Entrance Examination Board, New York, NY.

Page 34 art reprinted with permission of T/Maker Graphics Co., 2115 Landings Dr., Mountain View, CA 94043

INDEX